My Haunted Life

Extreme Edition

G. Michael Vasey

To all people who spend their nights scared silly...

And for my kids – Paul, Liam, Jon and Denisa

Foreword

Welcome to the extreme version of the hit Kindle series of books of short, but true, tales of the supernatural and paranormal. Essentially, this paperback is all three Kindle collections combined along with two entirely new and bonus stories at the end.

The project started as an attempt to document my ghostly and supernatural experiences growing up, but with the success of My Haunted Life, I ended up writing two more volumes. The latter two volumes were the result of pestering my friends and colleagues for their strange stories. I apologize to them for being such a pain! In the process, I recalled a few additional personal experiences as well.

Almost all the stories in this book are absolutely true. One is not true. One story is a work of fiction that came to me on a train to Budapest one evening. As I watched the eastern European landscape pass by, I started to think about the tales of vampires that originated in Hungary and Romania and the story was written there on the train.

Thanks for purchasing this book and I do hope it makes you think about the nature of this miracle we call reality and about our role within it.

Brno, March, 2015

Introduction

My childhood was a strange one. One of my first memories is of a little, blue man who emerged out of a mirror in my bedroom, shot me with a toy gun and then jumped out of the window into the backyard below. You might perhaps think that I imagined it, except for the fact that my parents actually heard the gunshot!

It didn't get better. In many ways, it got worse; but before I continue, though, with my story, let me digress just a little.

Row, row, row your boat,
Gently down the stream.
Merrily, merrily, merrily, merrily,
Life is but a dream.

I recall singing that song when I was a small child and wondering what did it mean? – *Life is just a dream?*

Where did this rhyme come from, and who wrote it? A bit of research suggests that the earliest printing of it was back in 1852, but who actually wrote it and why now seems lost in the mists of time. If anyone knows, please do let me know…

I thought life was a dream, too, when I was a child; or rather, I thought it a virtual reality game that I controlled, and I was sat in a box-like room connected to a machine that gave me vision and senses. So to be honest, I didn't puzzle too much over the idea that life might be a dream. I rather accepted that it almost certainly was.

I have lost so much as I have grown, and yet I have also gained so much. My imagination as a child was beyond equal. I could create other worlds right there in my head, and my dreams and my waking life seemed interconnected and one. I could fly back then. Magic—physical magic—was real, and so were elves. There was the girl I loved so much, who I dreamed about over and over again, trapped on an island of towering cliffs and looked after by her wicked witch of an aunt. One dream ran into the next, even weeks apart, until I finally rescued my love, and the wicked witch met her destiny.

We may have unlimited imagination as children, but there is no experience of real life. Unfortunately, as we grow older and supposedly wiser, we lose much of that ability unless we work on it. It's as if we build ourselves a prison.

It begins with our parents who, knowing no better, burden us with a lot of their beliefs, fears and worries. Next, it's other kids (peer pressure) and our teachers (culture, way of seeing things, etc.). We lose our ability to just imagine, and it is replaced instead with the straight jacket that is normality and acceptance. We no longer 'row the boat, gently down the stream,' but rather fight the currents going in God knows which direction and to what end? Oblivion?

Life loses its innocence, its gaiety, its merriness. It's no longer a dream but a nightmare.

That is until you re-remember how to imagine. Re-learn how to center yourself, imagine and dream again. The combination of childish imagination skills and the adults' experiences of life to at first remember to row, gently DOWN the stream (with the current), go with the flow, merrily understanding that it is YOUR dream, and you can create your own reality.

So, as you read my short stories about some of the strange, paranormal and downright creepy things that happened in my haunted life, ask yourself this question: Was this real, my imagination or maybe a bit of both?

The Visitor

It was some strange time in the morning
So early it was still night and without sunlight
The air was so cold, and you could hear a pin drop
I shivered involuntarily and tried to sleep
But there it was again
The deepest of sighs rattling like a death breath
My blood ran cold
I strained to listen, hearing the loudness of total silence
But there it was again
A scraping rustling sound scratching along the hallway
My heart palpitated
At any moment now, that door will begin to open
At any moment now, I will scream with all my lungs
And there will be nothing there
Nothing there at all
And I will lay and pray
That the morning sun rises soon illuminating my room
And ensuring that my ghostly visitor stays away
Throughout the day

*Originally published in the Moon Whispers collection
of poetry by G. Michael Vasey*

Seeking Neverland

As a young child, I think I was actually quite an innocent. Perhaps I was a tad over-protected by my parents, or perhaps I was just wired that way. To be honest, I do not know. I do know, though, that I had (and to some degree still do have) an imagination. My imagination was so strong that I constantly drew other children into my fantasyland, and when I left that fantasy, even momentarily, they stopped playing there, too. It was as if I were the catalyst for whatever fantasy we built. It was I who built layer upon layer of substance out of sticks, dustbins, stones and such. I would often delay having to go to the bathroom simply because I knew that on my return, the fantasy would be lost, gone, over. Looking back, it was if I created and wove the dance we danced in my childhood reality. And perhaps I did.

I dreamed well, too. Better then than now. Lucid dreaming, something I find difficult these days, came naturally to me then. I would willfully continue a dream, night after night, picking up right where I recalled leaving off. One dream was about a girl. She lived in a castle-like house on an island. It was a small island with steep cliffs all around, and it started as I found a cave and worked my way up to find the house.

The house had tall, forbidding stone walls and was partially fortified with archer turrets on each corner. Looking in through a window, I saw a girl. She was beautiful, and I fell in love with her as soon as my eyes saw her. She was my age in the dream—six or seven, perhaps. She looked so very sad, and I wondered how such a pretty girl living in such a magnificent house could be so sad?

One day, she caught sight of me. We made signs and faces through the window. She even smiled, but she kept looking around nervously. She would shoo me away at times, and I would hide and spy as a witch-like lady entered the room, and the girl would cry. I eventually discovered that the witch-like lady was an evil old hag who practiced black magic in the basement and caves below the house. She abused the girl who was her niece. I discovered the girl's parents had died, leaving her in the care of this wicked aunt. As the dream continued, the girl would secretly let me in, and we would play happily in that room until the aunt came. Then I would hide or leave, or hide and then leave, my heart pounding like a drum.

In the end, I was, of course, discovered and caught. The girl and I were taken to the basement, and we were tied up. Somehow, we escaped and turned the tables on the wicked witch, ridding the world of her via her own evil magic once and for all. The girl was free. She was happy and smiled, and we would play until, eventually, the dreams stopped.

These dreams took place over an extended period of time, and if you analyze them they have elements of all fairy tales, don't they? The wicked witch, the sad and mistreated niece or stepdaughter, and the prince who frees the girl and, in the end, marries her. The prince is the part of me that faces and confronts something within me—the evil, old witch—and defeats it in order to reconcile other aspects of myself.

When I look back now at my childhood, I wonder at how magical it really was. I wonder at the abilities I seem to have lost or misplaced as I have grown older and become a part of another world. Imagination is a precious commodity, and the art of dreaming is a wonderful and magical tool to heal oneself. I am convinced at times that I really lost something growing up, something truly magical. Some gift I was born with. Perhaps we all have.

You see, the problem is that, *"The moment you doubt whether you can fly, you cease forever to be able to do it."*

JM Barrie's Peter Pan has some interesting quotes throughout in my opinion that now resonate both with me and the World that I live in. Just consider the following, and perhaps you will agree.

"Never say goodbye because goodbye means going away and going away means forgetting."

"You know that place between sleeping and awake, that place where you can still remember dreaming? That's where I'll always think of you."

"All the world is made of faith, and trust, and pixie dust."

The thing I miss about being a child is my Peter Pan. Every one of us has a Peter Pan within us, and we lose him growing up. Some of us never realize it nor care, but others, like me, keep looking and searching for Neverland, knowing that not only does it exist, but I once went there all of the time.

The Cavalier

We lived in a typical semi-detached house on the outskirts of Hull. So far as I know, it was built in the 1920s, and it had little history that might make you think it could be haunted. I recall my first impressions of the place, though, as a young boy. It was cold with no central heating, felt damp and gloomy, and the bare floorboards and old wallpaper added a creepiness to the place. Of course, my dad was an amazingly resourceful man, and very soon, the entire place was redecorated and central heating added. Still, it always had an atmosphere so far as I was concerned.

It wasn't long after moving in that my worst fears were confirmed. I shared a room with my brother, Chris. On the other wall, our father had built fitted cupboards with a desk in between for homework. One night, as I peeked out from under the bedclothes, I saw a white outlined type of figure sat close to where the desk was, scribbling away. The figure wore a broad-brimmed hat and was dressed like a Cavalier. Not being the bravest of souls, after recovering from the shock, I screamed. Chris awoke or stirred at the sound of that, and we both watched as the figure turned its head, disturbed, stood up and then glided over and out through the wall. Chris still recalls the incident as well as I.

A few years later, we were camping in the caravan at Hawkeshead in the Lake District. As we walked back from the town to the campsite a couple of miles away, it was already dark. As Dad, his friend Jack, me and my brothers, and Jack's daughters were walking in almost pitch black down a country road, we heard the distant sound of a horse, its hoofs thudding along as it ran very quickly from somewhere behind us. I recall watching the horse and its highwayman-type rider pass us by as if oblivious of the road, the drystone walls, the trees, anything, or us. It simply travelled through things as opposed to around them! The thudding of the horse's hoofs got louder as it passed us by, but there was no doubting among those of us who had seen it—it was a ghostly rider we had just seen.

Many years later, I was traveling with my consulting job back and forth to quite a posh village near Manchester—I forget its name now. I was doing a project at a large bank, actually on the very first ATM machines to be deployed around the country by the bank. I stayed at a variety of different hotels, but there was one in the center of town that I stayed at a few times, which was haunted. It had an original central core and then a newly-built wing. I had no problems at all in the newly-built wing; but one night, arriving later, I was allocated a room in the original part of the hotel. I had no clue as to what was about to happen, but the room was oak paneled, and I thought it very grand. I got into bed more or less straight away and began to read—I recall it was a book by Israel Regardie. I began to feel watched. It was a very weird feeling, but it was as if something were watching me. Little knocks and scrapes started to happen, and shadows seemed to move around the room with no origin. I never did see a ghost, but the noises and moving shadows got worse and worse. The end for me came when the bedclothes were slowly and deliberately pulled off me, and the room became very chilly. I packed my bag and went to the reception to request a room change. The man there didn't seem at all surprised. I found out the next day that the older part of the hotel was reputed to be haunted.

Over the years, I have become better at blocking out things, and it is a rare occurrence now to have such an experience. Despite that, when my brother first moved into his house years ago, I had to tell him after my first visit that that there was a little, old man sharing the house with him, and it didn't like him being there. I understand that they did have a few strange experiences there in the first few years.

I have always had a sort of morbid fascination for ghosts, and I love a good ghost story. I'd just rather not be *in* the story.

Family Bible

"Come and look at this," my father said with a tone in his voice I recognized as meaning it was something interesting.

I walked over to our kitchen table curiously. He had a book. It was actually a huge book and leather-bound.

"It's a Bible," explained my dad.

It was a large and heavy, black, leather-bound Bible. It looked quite old, too.

"It belonged to neighbors of mine when I was a boy," explained Dad, leafing through some of the pages. "Here, look at this."

The inside cover of this huge family Bible was written in, and once I got used to the old fashioned handwriting, I realized it was a four-generation family tree. Did it mark the path this Bible had taken through the family?

As if answering my mental question, Dad told me that the Bible had been acquired in the 17th century and passed down through several generations of the family. That family was now extinct. It had died out with the recent death of the old lady who had given Dad this Bible for safekeeping.

I found this Bible fascinating. It's age, the smell of the paper, the strange typeface used, the binding and leather cover that was embossed in a strange design. It was a mysterious book in many respects.

We examined the book for quite a while, and then my father packed it in paper and took it up to the attic where it would stay at least for the time being. We thought nothing more of that Bible.

In the days and weeks that followed, strange things began to happen in the house. It started with creaks and groans, unexplained bangs and crashes from the attic. "Just the heating and cooling of the rafters," my Dad told us reassuringly. But things didn't improve, and if anything, steadily got worse. Nights were filled with strange sounds and sudden crashes that woke us all up. Added to some of the other things that I was experiencing at the time, it meant I hardly slept due to fear. I would lie there waiting for the sounds to start, and then when they did, I grew more and more jumpy and afraid as they continued throughout the night.

Unfortunately, however, other sounds began to emerge from the attic. Deep sighs that sounded as if the most depressed person you had ever met just let out their last death rattle. Then there were the slow, dragging footsteps punctuated with those horrible deep sighs of despair and followed by a few more footsteps.

I wasn't the only one hearing these sounds every night, and I met my father on one or two occasions, armed with a flashlight heading up the vertical pull-down ladder into that little square hole in the roof at the top of the stairs. He was investigating those sounds, although mostly he just muttered something about me getting back to bed.

The sounds were truly scary. Imagine if every night it sounded like someone or something was slowly moving around your attic amongst crashes and creaks, sighs and groans. The hairs stood up on the back of my neck hearing those sounds as the cold hands of fear seemed to clasp around my neck, slowly strangling me.

As abruptly as the noises started, they stopped. I noticed almost immediately and finally slept. No noises that night nor the next or the next. In fact, the noises were gone and never returned.

It was only several years later, when I happened to be talking to my dad about the noises, that an explanation emerged.

"It was that bloody Bible. I am sure of it," said my father, somewhat to my surprise.

"Bible? You mean that big family Bible you showed me that day?" I asked.

"Yes, that one. It always did give me a bad feeling, and that family never really liked us, so I had wondered why we were given it. One night, I went up in the attic and found the damn thing. I took it down, placed it in one of those old biscuit tins, and then the next day, I buried it at the bottom of the garden. Seemed to work," he added, looking at me with a grin.

Who knows if it was that Bible or what the sounds really were, but one thing is for sure. If you one day happen to dig up an old biscuit tin containing an old, leather family Bible, throw it away as quickly as you can.

Just a Game?

If there is one game that most certainly is *not* a game, it is the Ouija board. I have avoided that board like the plague most of my life. However, one night, in my late teens, my friend and I went to visit an ex-teacher of his. Well, actually, we went on the pretext of visiting her, but actually, it was her daughter we really went to see. That really is, as they say, another story.

It was quite late by the time we arrived. We had already been for a beer at the pub and then had the idea to visit as we drove home. Their house was a huge home in a well-to-do area outside Hull. It was four stories and must have been well over a hundred years old. A beautiful home.

Inside, we were told that the daughters were playing a board game in the kitchen with some friends. One look told me all I needed to know. It was an Ouija board.

"No, that's not for me," I said immediately.

My friend decided to join them, and so I sat next door in the TV lounge with the teacher, and we watched a movie in near silence. I guess about forty minutes had passed when I heard pandemonium suddenly break loose from next door. The door opened, and my friend came running out, through the room, out into the hallway and up the stairs followed by the girls. We were stunned. My friend was streaming tears, sobbing as he ran. For the next five minutes or so, we all chased him around the house. He sobbed and ran; we chased. It was simply bizarre behavior.

In the end, it was I who caught him on the stairs. By now, I suspected that someone or something was in control of my friend and, as my arm caught him on the staircase, I said, "Come into me."

I don't remember much of what happened after that. Apparently, the entity took my invitation to heart and did indeed enter me with the result that I, too, started running around the house, sobbing, being chased by everyone. After around thirty minutes of this, I 'woke up' at the bottom of the staircase with wet cheeks and a bunch of concerned faces all staring down at me.

It would seem that the family thought that their house was haunted by a specific entity, and in the kitchen, they had started to try to converse with this entity. Thinking that the conversation was simply one of them playing games with the others, my friend had demanded the entity 'prove it' with stunning results. Apparently, the entity was looking for something that it felt it had lost and was searching the house, crying as it searched. Somehow, both my friend and then I had tapped into this and began to exhibit the same behavior.

The funny thing is that I do not recall anything of that thirty or so minutes. It is as if I had vacated the premises for that entire time. Though, where I went while the entity used my body, I do not know. It only confirmed my suspicions that Ouija boards are best left well alone.

Poltergeist

Growing up in my house was, on the whole, pretty good. We had great parents, almost every weekend we were gone camping somewhere, we had two proper holidays each year, and I have no complaints at all. Just a bunch of heartfelt thanks to my parents, and a growing sense of awe as to how they did all that with three small boys and not a lot of money.

When I was eleven, we moved. It was a good move to be honest from a terraced three up, two down in west Hull, to a rather nice semi-detached outside of Hull. It meant a better school and a nicer environment back then. It stretched my parents' finances a bit, too. It is funny, though, that my brothers and I really did not like that house the first time we saw it. It had terrible wallpapers, it was gloomy and ill lit, very cold and damp without central heating. Between the three of us, there was no excitement at moving there.

Of course, within a few months, that house was completely different. Central heating had been installed, old fireplaces blocked up and replaced with modern gas fires, new wallpaper and décor and new curtains. To make it seem more homely, a couple of internal windows had been added, letting much more light enter into the rooms as well. It was transformed. All was well in the Vasey household; but it wasn't to stay that way.

The first incident was the Cavalier ghost, and after that, I swapped rooms with my little brother giving me the smallest bedroom at the front of the house but also the privacy of my own room. I gradually came to loath that room. It started with the noises—strange noises at all times of day—but mostly in the dead of night. Scrapping sounds and scratching sounds. Dad put it down to maybe a squirrel in the loft. I wasn't as convinced.

Things would also move around. I would place my watch by the bathroom sink to get washed and find it in the kitchen. At first, I thought it was Dad having fun as he was always a great practical joker; but it soon became apparent that it was not him. Keys went missing. Money, too. These would then, just as mysteriously, turn up in the strangest places like on a window ledge or under the sofa cushions.

The next developments were what eventually had me relieved to leave and go to college. It was what kept me awake at night in total fear. Have you noticed that silence is loud? I mean, when you are really, really focused on listening to nothing, it is very, very loud. I would lie in bed, head under the bedclothes, bedside light on, listening. The scratting sounds, scratching sounds and the sounds of doors opening that I knew were locked, the sounds of footsteps and breathing. It was enough to make the hair stand up on the back of your neck.

I would actually dread coming home from college for a weekend or the summer because of this. By the way, this only happened when I was there! Just for me, apparently. I would literally go out and get drunk in order to stay there. The best example was one night close to Christmas. I was home from college and had been out with my friend and had a few. I was sleeping on the floor in my brother's room that night. I lay down, hoping to pass right out, but instead, I was cold stone sober and scared half to death by the sound of the front door opening. Now, the first thing I thought was that somehow I had left the door unlocked, but I knew that wasn't the case as I had checked it on the way up the stairs. The key was in the lock, and that door was locked.

The front door opened and closed as I listened, sitting half up in bed. There was a deep sigh and a little cough. Ice-cold fear ran through my veins. The silence was so loud it was unbearable. Then, the first footstep and creak of the bottom stair. My heart was beating as if to burst. Another long sigh and another step. And another. I was now fumbling for the light, but my hands were shaking so hard I couldn't find it. By now, the steps seemed to be at the top of the stairs and moving along the hallway. The floorboards creaked, and there was that sigh again. I was frozen to the spot, but what I actually wanted to do was run. Run anywhere. There was a moment's silence, and then I watched in disbelief and horror as the bedroom door began to slowly swing open.

I screamed. I screamed so loudly you probably heard me in London.

A few moments passed by, and then the door flew open. There, to my utter relief, stood my dad in his pajamas holding a very large spanner in one hand and a flashlight in the other. He switched on the light, and my brother looked about him in a state of shock through two sleepy-looking eyes.

"It's okay. I heard that, too," said my dad. "I heard it, too."

We sat, Dad and my brother and I, for quite a while, but all was quiet. Whatever it was, it had gone. I eventually fell asleep, and my dad went back to bed, checking the doors in the process.

We didn't talk much about it the next day. It was simply something that happened in that house when I was home. My dad said it was poltergeist activity, and it was centered around me. I think he was right. We didn't really know what to do about it, but we did discover one thing. If I got angry, the phenomena stopped. So, that is what I would do. I would get angry and shout at whatever it was to get lost or perhaps use even more choice phrases. If a door started to open, instead of screaming, I pulled the door open with a verbal challenge. It had the desired effect.

The activity followed me, though. It followed me to Aston University until I met Anantha. But that is another story.

A Meeting with God

A few weeks into my college days, as I made my way from the Students' Union building to my student flat on the nineteenth floor of a campus building, I noticed a rather suspicious looking character who seemed to be following me around. As I entered one of the elevators in the ground floor of the building, he followed, peering sideways at me but looking away whenever I tried to catch his eye. As the elevator arrived at my floor, I was hoping it was all just my imagination and that perhaps he would continue up to the top floor above me. But, as I left the elevator, he followed, and as I reached the doorway into the group of six study bedrooms, shared kitchen, and bath that was my home on campus, he was still right there—right behind me.

"Do you want something?" I asked nervously.

"Gary, I want to talk to you," he said quietly.

"How do you know my name?" I asked in surprise.

"Oh, I know a lot about you," he replied. "And I must speak with you—now, if possible."

Reluctantly, I let him into my study bedroom, and he

introduced himself as an Indonesian student. He practiced meditation, he said, and he had been asked by his Guide to talk to me and help with some challenges that I was facing. I was rather incredulous but convinced. How exactly did he know my name?

Anantha and I actually became firm friends from that point forward. He really did know a lot about me for someone I had just met, and that seemed both mysterious and alluring. He tried to help me understand that I was a 'sensitive' and that this sensitivity meant that I was open to all the flotsam and jetsam of the astral world. He also told me that my uncontrolled reaction—pure fear—was attracting things from that realm that I was probably better off without. He started to teach me some psychic self-defense methods that were useful; but the problem was that at the smallest hint of any phenomenon, I became a total wreck, and fear possessed me completely.

In order to help me overcome this deep-seated fear, he suggested that it might help if I could share a controlled experience with him. Sitting me down in a comfortable position, he asked me to close my eyes and relax. Peeking out of the corner of my eye, I watched him do likewise. Suddenly, I was with him in a stone tunnel. It seemed to go on for a great distance, and as it did so, it slowly curved around so that you could not see where the tunnel went. What I could see, though, was the brightest light I have ever seen. It filled the tunnel with golden light, but its source was always just around the bend so that it could not actually be seen directly. The light began to fill me with laughter. It made me feel very happy; happier than I had ever felt, and happier than anyone has any right to feel. I began to laugh out loud, and as I did so, tears of joy sprang from my closed eyes. As I laughed, an odd thing happened. My laughter seemed to become magnified thousands of times and to descend in pitch until I realized that this was not my laughter anymore but someone or something else's laughter. The laughter permeated throughout my entire being so that everything was laughter and golden light, and I knew then that I was in the presence of God.

When I finally came out of the trance that I had found myself in, Anantha was already sitting opposite me with a smile on his face and a questioning look in his eyes.

"You see, He is always there for you," he explained. "There is no need to be frightened. All you have to do is trust in Him."

As I've discovered on several occasions since then, a wonderful experience like that quickly fades, just as the memory of a dream fades. At the time that it happens and shortly afterwards, it feels as if it should surely stay with you forever, but it fades just the same as consciousness returns to normality. And, with its fading away, so too the newly found and almost grasped confidence goes with it. As Anantha left, I was ashamed to feel just as frightened as I had been before.

Anantha did help me a lot, though. Through slow perseverance, he got me to a state that I could best describe as the toleration of fear. He was also someone with whom I could share my thoughts and experiences without fear of reproach or that look of horror as your confidant realizes that you might well be a total freak. Unfortunately, he left the college at the end of my first year returning to Indonesia, and I never heard from him again.

The Green Blob and the Skeletal Priest

Before he left, Anantha showed me that the dream world could be used to help me. I was experiencing repetitive nightmares about a big green blob with evil red eyes that pursued me tirelessly each night, even into my waking state. I am sure that the writers of Ghostbusters must have experienced the same thing because when I watched the movie a few years later—there was my green blob, sliming everyone!

"See, I told you," he said. "Your fear is attracting things you really don't need. But there is something you can do about this."

In describing my nightly tormentor to him, I mentioned an amulet that was attached to a gold chain worn around the blob's neck. He told me that I should properly prepare before bedtime and then try to sleep. When I started to dream, I should summon up the courage to confront the blob and break off the amulet from the chain and keep it.

"The amulet represents the entity's hold on you. If you can break the chain, you will be free of it finally," he explained.

31

I wasn't sure that I could control a dream in this way, but I tried. It worked. I was able to do exactly as he said in the dream that night, and the blob was gone for good.

"Good job," said Anantha, listening to my story the next day. "But the next one will be much, much harder."

"Next one?" I whispered.

"Yes, the next one," said Anantha.

The 'next one' duly appeared more or less as soon as Anantha had departed for Indonesia. Sitting in my student flat late one evening, I became aware of that now familiar uneasy feeling in the pit of my stomach and coldness at the back of my neck. I stood bolt upright and began to sweat. The walls of my flat seemed to simply vanish, and I could see the entire city of Birmingham from my vista. In the distance was a terrible figure. Clothed in the purple regalia of a churchman, it seemed to be fighting against an unseen wind to get closer to me. I began to use some of the self-defense techniques I had been shown, but clumsily, as I was panicking. The figure was now so close to me that I could see its appalling face—a skull with dark eye sockets—grinning and leering at me, arms flailing in my direction as it sought to move closer. How long this lasted, I have no idea; but a rap at the door broke the spell, and the room came rushing back.

I slept little that night. The knock at the door turned out to be Brendan, my friend and flat mate. He had sensed that something odd was happening and had arrived to investigate. I explained my predicament, and Brendan, an Irish Catholic, started to draw crosses on each wall of my room with a pencil. We sat together, chatting through most of the remainder of the night. I was moving out the next day; my first year of college was over. Goodness knows what the university made of my room after I had left with its penciled crosses on each wall!

Throughout that summer and for the remainder of my college days in Birmingham, the skeletal priest plagued me on and off. The effect was to make me more fearful and jumpy than at any time in my life. But life was bearable, especially when I was able to take my mind off the priest-like specter.

The Last Supper

At the beginning of my second year of college, I moved into a flat in West Bromwich. It was quite a distance from the university, but it was the only thing I could find that I could afford. There was a bus ride into Birmingham, and so I just had to get used to the idea of commuting.

At some point, I had acquired a very large paper poster of Leonardo da Vinci's Last Supper. I really liked the painting and would often spend time studying the detail of the picture. It hung proudly on the main wall of the flat.

One evening, I went out and ended up at a party. I met a girl there who was an art student. We got talking, and I mentioned that I wrote poetry and song lyrics. She talked to me about how she was expected to paint and create a group of art items around a theme for a project. Somehow, we arrived at the idea that perhaps she would use my poetry for that. The only thing left to do was for her to review the poems, so we made arrangements for her to visit the following Saturday afternoon.

On Saturday morning, when it finally arrived, I tried to tidy and clean the flat. I was quite keen to impress her, if the truth be told. I even went out and bought a few small cakes from the bakery and spent a small fortune on some decent instant coffee. She duly arrived, and she sat opposite me across a small table. In between munching on the cakes, she began to read some of my poetry[1]. At once, she spotted the theme that we had discussed and that had initially piqued her interest— fear, ghosts, astral plane and so on.

"Why do you write so many on that set of topics?" she asked.

I tried my best to explain. I told her about the Cavalier ghost, the activities at my house that had followed me to West Bromwich, about my interest in understanding it all and my avid reading of books on magic and the esoteric.

She laughed. "That's a load of bloody nonsense," she giggled.

---

[1] The best works of my poetry from this era was published as Weird Tales in 2006.

To be honest, I was a bit angered by that reaction. She sat there, reading my innermost secrets in those poems, and when I explain what motivated them, she laughed!

"No, it isn't nonsense. Not at all," I said firmly.

"Of course, it is. There are no such things as ghosts," she said matter-of-factly. "Magic is something done on stage by people using trickery."

"No, you are wrong."

"Prove it," she said.

Those two words—prove it—damn it, I would try. I was pretty angry at having my intelligence questioned and being insulted by a person who plainly had never experienced anything at all unusual. Prove it, indeed.

I began mentally repeating the words, "Make something happen—prove it to her." I didn't really expect anything to happen, to be honest. I had not really ever tried to make something happen as, honestly, I was too scared of what might occur if I were successful. Anger and indignation, pride and ego this time, however, motivated me to try. There was no technique, no magic words, just a deep-seated will driven by anger to make her eat those words.

"I will," I said forcefully.

To my utter amazement, the windows behind me suddenly rattled and with a loud cracking noise, blew wide open. A rush of air entered the flat, blowing her hair back and scattering the pile of poems all around the room. Her eyes, probably like mine, widened in total shock and awe. Then, the *pièce de résistance*, the huge, paper Leonardo da Vinci Last Supper picture, pinned to the wall with pins, suddenly billowed off from that wall behind her, passed over her head and landed on the coffee table in front of her. It actually flew *against the wind* from the window to get there.

There was a moment's silence as she surveyed and computed what had just occurred. White as a sheet, she leapt to her feet, clutched her belongings and ran out of the door. I never saw her again.

I, too, was shocked. Actually, scared silly might be more accurate.

I really do not know what happened that afternoon. Did I really cause that to happen, or was it simply just a freakish coincidence that at the moment I willed something to happen, a strong wind blew open the windows of the flat? It had never happened before, and it never happened again. I guess I will never know. It was, however, a long time before I ever tried to work magic again.

The Sword and The Water

The Island of Eigg is a small island south of the Isle of Skye in the Inner Hebrides of Scotland. It was the place I chose to go and spend six weeks doing geological mapping for my undergraduate thesis. I had written to the laird seeking permission and had been duly given that permission along with instructions on where I could camp.

The Island of Eigg at that time had about fifty inhabitants living on it, either permanently or just for summer work for the estate. Most of these people lived in the southern part of the island, however, and most of my work would take place in the northern portion where the geology was more varied and interesting.

My father had built a large box with wheels at the back and a pulling handle at the front. In it, I packed two tents, camping gear, tinned and packet food and everything else I thought might be needed. The box was shipped in advance so as to arrive before me. I followed the box a week or so later, taking the train first to Glasgow and then along the 'Harry Potter' route from Glasgow to Mallaig. Once in Mallaig, I took the Ferry to Eigg with my box and other possessions.

Needless to say, the trip from Glasgow to Mallaig is magnificent. There is lots of beautiful scenery to view almost the entire trip. On arrival, I was rather surprised to discover that my box was on the same train, and I realized just how fortunate I was. Had it arrived a day later, what on earth would I have done? The box and I moved to the ferry that was a smallish boat with about twenty or so other people aboard. Approaching Eigg, I thought that the island resembled a huge tanker at sea. The rock formations of lava plateaus and the huge Sgur of Eigg at one end give it a very interesting profile.

On arrival, I knew I would pull that box a few miles across the island. I hadn't anticipated how heavy the box was as I pulled it up the winding hill, sweating and cursing as I did so. A few cars passed me by, but no one offered to help. At the top, I rested a while and then began again, pulling the box a couple of miles and then down the other side of the island into a bay where I would camp. I hadn't seen a soul in a couple of hours by the time I arrived at the designated campsite. In fact, I didn't see anyone for a couple of days!

The campsite was on the location of an old monastery, and me being me, I was a bit creeped out by it. The first tent blew down the first night in a gale, and my spare tent broke a pole the next day. I was essentially screwed. No place to stay and over five weeks of work to be done. I spent the remainder of the day visiting a few scattered cottages in that area asking if anyone could put me up and eventually found a man who had an old caravan in a field and would rent that to me for the five weeks. I moved in feeling pretty good. It was more comfortable and roomy than my tent, and it was quite a way from the old monastery site.

I started my field mapping in earnest, exploring the island, collecting samples, describing the rocks and so on. I was totally alone in very remote locations almost all day long every day. I honestly didn't see anyone in three entire weeks until I ran out of certain foods and had to walk several miles back to the other end of the island to buy provisions.

Being surrounded by nature and not talking to people actually is quite pleasant after a while. You learn to keep your own company and occupy your thoughts. I found myself thinking aloud for the sake of hearing a voice at times. Nights seemed long, and being of a nervous disposition, I often slept poorly, listening to the wind howling through the ropes that held down the caravan and other strange noises. From time to time, I was really frightened by a strange noise that would occur in the middle of the night. The caravan would move from side-to-side and vibrate while the noise occurred. I would simply lie there, terrified, with my flashlight in one hand and geological hammer in the other.

From time to time, I would hear (or did I imagine?) a sort of strange, harmonic singing. It would rise in intensity and then fade away again. When it occurred, I would, of course, stand and try to establish where it was coming from. The sheep, about the only other living creatures around, stared back at me, munching grass, probably thinking me mad. Over a period of several days, this singing became louder and happened more often. I was convinced someone was just over the hill with a radio or something, but I never saw anyone. It wasn't creepy. In fact, it was beautiful, peaceful and almost a religious experience listening to this harmonic singing.

A few days later, I found myself mapping a small gorge with extremely interesting geology. As I was tapping away at some rocks, I heard the singing yet again, but this time very loudly. I was in the bottom of the gorge, and a small but active stream bubbled through and over rocks with small waterfalls along the way. Steep cliffs rose either side of me. I turned around, quite jarred by the sudden, loud sound, and there she was. Halfway up the other cliff on a ledge was a most beautiful woman dressed in blue. She had dark hair pinned up in a sort of bun and a broad smile on her face as she looked down at me. I stood with mouth agape staring back at her.

Who was she, and how on earth had she gotten halfway up the cliff? I asked myself. I wasn't afraid at all; in fact, I felt real peace and tranquility emanating from her. I guess the vision lasted a few minutes at most, and then the woman began to fade along with the angelic choir singing the accompaniment. I actually spent sometime looking for her just to make sure that it wasn't one of the people on the island having fun with me. I didn't find any trace of anyone. I then sat and meditated and prayed for a while, as it seemed like a real, religious-type experience.

The next day, I was sitting on the beach eating my lunch when the singing began again. It got louder and louder and much more intense over a short period, and then it happened. Out past the rocks, an arm rose from the water holding a sword. The music and singing reached fever pitch, and it seemed as if there was just the singing, the sword and me. To be honest, I started to giggle. I mean, it was so absurd—so Arthurian, so ridiculous—I had to laugh. I also had a crack at reaching the sword, but I couldn't get there. After a few minutes, the arm disappeared with the sword beneath the waves and the singing began to fade. Again, I was left in sort of quasi-religious state wondering what on earth I was experiencing and even suspecting that my lack of company was beginning to send me quite mad.

Whatever the lady and the arm with the sword were, I didn't see them again, although I looked. I did hear the singing, and I heard it quite a lot, but always in the distance. If something had meant to transpire, I had missed my opportunity. I often wonder what that was all about. Was it simply my imagination, or was there really some message for me in what I saw there on Eigg?

As for the shaking of the caravan along with the accompanying sound, well, in the last week of my stay on Eigg, my dad joined me. I told him about this, and he listened. On the first night of his stay, it happened— the noise and the vibration of the caravan as it shook and moved side-to-side.

"See, Dad!" I said excitedly.

Dad flicked on his flashlight from the bed seat opposite me and got up. I heard him open the door. I was scared for him.

A minute or so later, I heard my father's laugh.

"Come and look at this, will you?" he shouted to me from outside the caravan, still laughing.

When I finally summoned up the courage to join him, I spotted the reason for his laughter and for my fear. A very large cow was rubbing its back against the rope that was holding the caravan down.

The Haunted Jacket

Many years ago, I was just a poor, broke student at a university in the U.K. At least back then, research students got the grants that allowed them to subsist and which could be supplemented with a bit of teaching or other part-time work. I was quite lucky in that I was teaching a geological mapping class to non-geology students for the amazing sum of ten pounds per hour, in addition to a subsistence grant from the NERC (if such a thing exists anymore). However, I can tell you, life wasn't easy financially!

Like most students back then, I also kept an eye on the second-hand clothes outlets for any bargains. One day, I spotted a beautiful tweed jacket that looked like it may fit me. I forget how much it was, but perhaps it was on sale for one pound or thereabouts. It was a sports jacket, something that would always go with a pair of jeans and t-shirt, and that would serve as an autumn coat at a push, too. It looked good on me and was almost a perfect fit. This was also surprising as I was very gangling—thin and tall with long arms and legs. Usually, if something was wide enough, it wasn't long enough and vice versa. Jeans were a particular problem—try looking for a 28" waist and 36" inside leg! Of course, these days, the waistline has progressively expanded, and I may just have shrunk a bit, too! Anyway, I digress. The jacket was a perfect fit, and it looked very good. I bought it.

I wore my new jacket that night. I had a date. As the evening wore on, however, my mood began to change. Initially happy and excited with the new jacket and that date, I began to become more and more morose as the evening wore on. I decided that it must be a combination of the weather (drizzling and dull) and perhaps one too many beers on an empty stomach. By the time I got home, I was feeling very agitated and depressed. It was as if a little cloud had formed over my head and was following me around.

The next day I was fine again. The day went quite well, and when I got home, I decided to do some grocery shopping and then go for a beer at the Students' Union. Of course, I wanted to look dapper, and so I put on my new jacket. The shopping proved to be very frustrating as a whole series of little problems emerged one by one, and by the time I got to the Students' Union, I was in a foul mood that got progressively worse as the evening wore on. My date from the previous evening joined me later, and she was very unimpressed by my mood— again! That little cloud was back and following me around again. She did, though, walk with me to my flat and accepted the offer of a coffee. I recall putting on the kettle but not much after that.

The slap was hard, and it was meant to be. It stung my cheek. I had no idea where I was or what I was doing. It was as if I hadn't been there at all. In fact, as it turned out, I wasn't. Someone else was, however, and my date was not particularly thrilled with this morose, verbally belligerent and semi-violent persona. As I tried to take in my surroundings and the anger of my date, I decided I was very confused. I guess at some stage, I took off that jacket and sat and discussed the incident with her. I told her I had blanked out, and she told me that I had essentially become someone else. My accent and voice had changed along with the look in my eye. I had started swearing, using words I would never use, and I had become threatening and not at all nice. It was as if I was a drunk she told me. I was puzzled. I had no memory of behaving that way—none at all.

"That jacket," she said, pointing to my beautiful new jacket.

"What about it?" I asked, somewhat puzzled.

"Every time you put that on, you change, and the longer you wear it, the worse you get."

I had to admit, it did seem that way.

I picked up the jacket and set it on my knee, meditating on it, and I knew abruptly that she was right. Whoever had owned that jacket was still wearing it. The jacket was, in a sense, haunted by the persona of its past occupant. I could, in fact, see him; and I realized that this alcoholic man had died recently and that his clothes had been sold in the second-hand store. I could sense him and his unpleasant odor, too. Why had I not seen or sensed that before?

The jacket went into a trashcan just as far away from my flat as possible.

I never bought second-hand clothes again.

The Voice

It was the summer of 1981. Bryan Adams was playing on the radio, the sun was shining and I was driving a brand new Ford Mustang. I was in Nova Scotia, Canada where I was doing my first season of fieldwork for my Ph.D. thesis. Things could not be better.

I had applied for a couple of Ph.D. programs earlier that summer. The one at Strathclyde University in conjunction with the British Geological Survey in Leeds was the one I wanted for all sorts of reasons. Firstly, it involved traveling to Nova Scotia; secondly, it was a topic that interested me; and finally, I thought, unlike many others that seemed designed to turn you into a university academic, this one might actually help me get a job. Even the trip for the interview had been fun as I left my parents caravanning with my brothers somewhere deep in the Yorkshire Dales and jumped on train to Glasgow. Back in 1981, this was still major travel, and I reveled in traveling. Prof. P. Mcl. Donald. Duff seemed a nice man, and we got along very well. I had a funny feeling I would get the gig, and I did with one proviso... I needed a driver's license, since otherwise getting about in Nova Scotia might be a serious issue.

Back at home, my father patiently instructed me in driving in the Mark 1 Ford Cortina he had purchased especially for the purpose—although, I do think he liked the car, too. I vividly recall the end of one lesson in which I had done quite well, and as I pulled up outside the house, Dad invited me to drive into the driveway. I tried. I took half the front brick wall with me, and later that night, listened guiltily from my bed as my father hammered the car back into some semblance of shape.

My driving test was booked, and there would be enough time to take a second attempt if necessary before my adventure to Nova Scotia began. I had a couple of proper lessons with a trained instructor, and he agreed that I was ready. Fingers crossed then. The problem as I now look back was opting to use the Ford Cortina to take the test. It was old, and it looked old. It was also sluggish to take off. I drove well, but still failed the test due to 'undue hesitation.' I was never sure whether it was me or the car that caused that, but yes, knowing the car, I was careful pulling out into the main road.

My second attempt was scheduled already, and I decided to use the much newer vehicle provided by my professional driving instructor. It was a good decision, and I drove straight through the test into a spanking new driver's license. I was now qualified to start the Ph.D. fieldwork.

I took the train to London, lugging a huge suitcase. I then took the tube to Heathrow and was really terrified I wouldn't make it on time. Of course, I did. I do not recall what sort of plane it was, but it had a standing bar at the front where you could drink and smoke. Bizarre. I had never flown before, and as the wheels left the ground, I wasn't sure if I really liked it either. A couple of gin and tonics later, I decided that I did.

I was met on arrival by the prof and his wife, and for the first week or so, he drove me around. At the end of that period, we went to the rental company and rented my car—a brand new, red Ford Escort. I couldn't believe it. I mean, what could possibly get better? Nova Scotia, brand new car and whole new world to explore…

The Escort lasted a day. On my first day on my own, I stopped for lunch at a burger joint. It had a front car park, and I pulled up, parked, pulled on the handbrake, got out, closed the door and stood watching as the car rolled slowly forward and then down a four foot drop into the front garden of the house next door! Apparently, in an automatic car, you are supposed to leave it in PARK, not neutral, and everyone knows that handbrakes are useless in automatic vehicles I was later told. Was it a premonition of things to come?

So, now you know how I ended up driving a 2-liter Mustang down a grit road in Nova Scotia. The only replacement that they could offer was that beauty, and let me tell you, it was a beauty. It went very well, and it looked great.

Off the main roads in Nova Scotia, at least back then, the roads are gravel and grit. So there I was, driving a beast of a car down a gravel road, Bryan Adams full blast on the radio, the sun streaming through the retractable top enjoying every second of this freedom. I was going very fast. Very, very fast indeed. Why not? It was fun.

"Gary—slow down!" said a voice behind me.

I swiveled around. The hairs on the back of my neck had jumped to attention, and my heart was beating like crazy. There was no one there. I slowed instinctively anyway since I was, as you might expect, very puzzled and just a little scared.

"SLOW DOWN!" said the voice again—louder this time.

I hit the brake quite hard in surprise and started to slow down abruptly. The tires spun in the gravel, and the car started to drift in a skid. I steered into it and around the hairpin bend that suddenly appeared in front of me. I just made it around that bend with one wheel hanging over the edge momentarily before the skid ended and the tires engaged again, pulling me to safety.

"Told you," said the voice behind me.

I stopped. I was shaking like a leaf. After a while, I got out, lit a cigarette with shaking hands and went back to the hairpin bend. It was a sheer drop, perhaps forty to fifty feet into a lake below. There had been no road sign, no warning, except for the voice. Had it not been for that voice, I would have been dead or badly injured in the lake below.

I think I looked like a ghost. What or who that miraculous voice was, I will never know. But it saved my life.

The Nightmare

A few nights ago, I was dreaming something, though now I cannot recollect what it was. I know that it was a long and continuous dream and that I was in a remote and beautiful place. I was revisiting it with my partner and child. The place was familiar and yet not. I recall thinking it was the Island of Eigg, but it was not—it was somewhere I have not been to in this reality. Anyway, I was walking down a rough lane between two flat fields of grass. My two companions were behind me a short distance.

Up ahead, I could see two figures: one an adult female and the other a child. As I saw them, it began to darken and to snow, and I was thinking that this was a tad strange. I continued to walk, and with the light fading, the weather changing and the two figures motionless, silhouetted in the distance, I began to feel a rising sense of ill. The feeling changed from one of worry to fear as I got closer to the two figures. The first was an overweight peasant-type woman simply dressed in a shawl with her hair inched back severely into a bun. She did not smile, and her skin was grimy. Her eyes seemed fixated on the distance behind me as if gazing miles and miles. The child was equally ragged and dirty, and as I approached, I noticed the child had black eyes. No white in those eyes—pure black. On seeing those eyes, the fear and dread within me reached a peak, and I began to float. As I floated over the top of the two figures, I was turning in the air, and my gaze was on the child's eyes. I was scared for myself but also for my companions who had lagged some distance behind me. At that moment, the child opened its mouth in a terrible scream, and that mouth opened so wide it could swallow me. I woke up, trembling, sweating and shouted, "No, No, No!"

It took me a good thirty minutes to rid myself of the feeling of doom, fear and indescribable horror of the dream.

An Old Man in Scotland

We were touring the west coast of Scotland for a day or two. We had set out from Glasgow that morning and fully intended to go back there that night, but the day had been fun with lots to see and do, and so by the time we entered Inverary, it was already quite late. In fact, we had already visited Inverary jail that morning before motoring a bit farther up the coastline, so the idea of staying the night there seemed a good one and would give us more time to look around.

In the end, we settled on the George in the main street and booked two rooms. My ex-wife and twin boys were allocated one room, while my elder son and I took the other. The twins were very taken with their room and excitedly showed me the oak paneling, portraits on the walls, four-poster bed complete with heavy curtains and the quaint but airy bathroom en suite that had an old fashioned bath on four legs. They thought it a great and funny room. I didn't like it. Not at all. I was relived to be sleeping down the hall in the more modern part of the hotel. Our room was normal with two side-by-side single beds separated by a small table and lamp.

By this time in my life, I had things more or less under control. It had been a long time since anything really strange had occurred, and at times, I rather missed that. That night, however, especially in that room, I felt the hair on the back of my neck stand up and a shiver go down my spine. I put it down to a draft, at least initially.

We ordered dinner in the bar and enjoyed a couple of beers, too. We couldn't really make it late because the twins were still fairly small and tired early in the evening. Reluctantly, it was soon time to go to bed, and off we all went up the staircase accordingly. Given my earlier discomfort and sixth sense that not all was quite normal with the hotel, I was uncomfortable.

I slept like a log. Really, I did. Nothing happened at all. I was relieved. At breakfast, I remarked that my ex-wife looked like she had had a bad night. She glared at me over tea and toast and said, "You have no idea!" The twins nodded in unison.

"What happened?" I asked.

"Dad, there was an old man, a nasty old man in our room," said one of the twins.

"Really?" I asked.

Apparently, they had got into the four-poster bed and switched on the TV. After a short while, they switched out the lights. Although all was okay until after they slept, my ex-wife said that she felt like someone was watching her. Later, they were woken by the bedclothes being pulled from the bed, and one of the twins swore that there was an old man in the room who didn't want them there. Noises and unexplained bangs occurred throughout the night, and eventually our son pointed at a portrait that was dimly visible on the wall and said, "It's that man, Mummy."

The portrait removed from the wall and turned to face it, they tried the best they could to sleep with the lights on. It wasn't much of a night's sleep for any of them by all accounts. There was an 'old man' odor in the room, too, I was told.

For once, it wasn't me who experienced bizarre things. Nonetheless, I had known there was something about that room, and I had said nothing. Not that it would have made any difference, I suppose.

Haunted Paintings

In fact, paintings sometimes feature strongly in paranormal activity. I will give two examples to prove my point.

The first is a story that my father told me a couple of times about his childhood. His mother was a *bonafide* medium, and he grew up with strange goings on just as I did. In fact, this is why he was sympathetic to my dilemma. Apparently, he and his family had once temporarily lived in a flat on the top floor of a three-story building. On the day that they were moving out, he recalled watching the comings and goings of people moving furniture and belongings. Eventually, all was complete, and he and his mother stood outside of their front door as she locked the apartment one last time.

"But Mum, what about this picture here," said my dad to his mother, pointing to the picture propped up against the wall at the top of the staircase.

His mother looked puzzled for a moment and then asked my dad who it was that he saw in that empty picture frame. My dad had always seen a little old man in the picture with eyes that followed him, and he was more than a little shocked to learn that there had *never* been any picture in that empty frame.

The second instance involves a week we spent in the family house of a friend in mid-Wales. He had inherited an estate complete with a sizable house by the coast. The house was 16th century, and on arrival, I knew it was haunted. There was no two ways about it. I could feel it, and it was with some trepidation that I knew we would spend a week here with friends and my parents.

The front entrance was into a large, gloomy and poorly lit hall. The darkness wasn't made any better by the dark wood paneling covering the walls. Frankly, it was creepy.

Things began to happen almost immediately. My parents complained about a sort of 'darkness' in their room that pulled their bedclothes off. They swapped to another bedroom. Apparently, that one wasn't much better either as the door kept opening by itself. Once again, nothing happened to me, though. I was in self-protect mode from the moment we arrived.

However, the creepiest incident yet again involved a portrait. Hanging halfway down the stairs in that creepy oak-paneled hall was the portrait of a man. To be honest, I barely noticed it, but our eldest son told us that when he had gone past it, its eyes followed him, and so he had stopped to look at it to see if he really was being watched by the painting. At this point, the head of the man in the portrait actually came out of the picture and spoke to him. Of course, he completely freaked out at this, as you might expect. Whether this was just a young and fertile imagination we will never know; but to him, it was a real and terrifying experience.

The entire week was punctuated with strange incidents, and on the last evening, we had a dinner party outside with the housekeepers who lived nearby on the estate. The conversation naturally turned to the experiences we had had, and they listened, nodding their heads. They had heard all of the stories before from other guests and experienced some themselves, too. The bedroom with the darkness, the portrait in the hall...

Reality Really Is Weird

I am reading an interesting book at the moment about the nature of reality. It has an interesting way of working its theme as it has you conducting experiments that will perhaps give you a different perspective on what is normal. This last two days, I have been doing one of the experiments where you simply look everywhere and expect to see something. In my instance, I decided that I would see a pink car. Don't ask me why. It just seemed like something fairly rare…

I actually finished reading the instructions on my Kindle, riding a bus to pick up my car from service. I decided on the pink car and looked up. As my eyes refocused on the view through the back window of the bus, I noticed another bus. It was white, but… it had huge pink stripes on it. I thought to myself, "Okay, that's not a car, nor is it totally pink, but that is pretty bloody weird!"

I got off the bus and had to walk back about a half-kilometer, and I was looking at all of the cars—parked, in motion, all of them. I realized that some reds had now begun to look pinkish to me, and then I saw it! Yes, a dark pink car went sailing past. In twenty-four hours, I saw two dark pink cars like that and one clearly 'pretty little girl' pink. Not only that, I began to notice pink everywhere. As I looked across a scene, pink items would jump up out of all the reality 'noise' in front of me. I saw pink writing, pink on billboards, pink houses, pink clothing, pink hair, pink ribbons... lots and lots of pink.

Now, let me tell you something. I have never, ever seen a pink car in Brno before. Never.

For the experiment, during the second twenty-four hours, you had to change it to something else... something living, perhaps... yes, an elephant. That's what I decided. I want to see an elephant. That was last night as I sat in front of the TV, and almost immediately as I looked up, yes, there was an elephant in a commercial as if right on cue. Later, watching a YouTube reel of funny cat videos (yep—you caught me doing that!), one had two baby elephants in it, too. Obviously, I didn't see a lot of elephants, but I did see some. Normally, I would not have done so. I mean, who sees elephants?

So, what does this prove?

Well, I think it proves that reality really is bloody weird.

It doesn't matter at this stage if by focusing on pink cars or elephants, I brought them into my reality or that by focusing and actively looking for something, I saw it. Both are stark results when it comes to reality. In the first, I really do create my reality by manifesting what I concentrate on; and in the latter, I manifest something that was already there but previously unnoticed by my consciousness. In the latter case, we receive so much data at any point in time, we must filter almost all of it out so that we only see what we are focused on seeing. If by focusing on something else, we now see this in the noise, then this proves something powerful, too. I mean, what ELSE are we NOT seeing because we DON'T know how to look for it?

I would say that in the above paragraph, if we create our own reality that is magic; but if by shifting our focus and noticing something that was always there but remained unseen, then that is magic, too.

You see, in magical training, much time and effort is dedicated to knowing ourselves. As we learn about ourselves, we become aware of aspects of ourselves we did not know about, we become focused on something we never saw before and we begin to try to change ourselves—to be more deliberate and less automated. As we do our magical training, some people may experience an increase in psychism, for example. Is this that person actually changing their outlook and changing what they chose to notice and now seeing something that was always there, but they never actually saw before?

I think so. Think about that for a minute, will you?

By the way, that book is called E Squared.

So the question is this: Did any of these strange paranormal events actually happen and did they happen because I was looking for them? Did I make them happen? Or was it all just a dream…?

Paranormal Phenomena

Ghosts, poltergeists, haunted clothing, haunted paintings, demons and the scary unexplained. In *My Haunted Life*, I recounted a number of stories of the strange and rather bizarre things that have happened to me in my life and they included all of the above. I then left readers with several questions about the nature of reality. *Had I brought these events into my reality simply by believing in them?*

The thing is, though, it isn't just me who experiences such weird paranormal phenomena, is it? A quick look over the news headlines for any random day will invariably include strange tales of ghosts, poltergeists, strange sightings, demons, possession, black-eyed kids and even more bizarre stories. It seems that the fear of the unknown, the strange, the dark and downright bizarre, is something that afflicts most of us. So, when we are alone at night in a spooky house after watching a scary movie, are we more susceptible to experiencing something paranormal?

It's interesting to note how a small child sees things. Many children have strange experiences, unseen friends and so on. As a child, the world seemed to be magical to me, but not in the way that all kids think the world magical when very young. No, I mean my world really *was* magical as evidenced by the dreams that I had and all of the strange things that I experienced. By the age of eleven or twelve, I was reading voraciously. While I will admit to the odd Enid Blyton book, most of the books that I read were by people like Madame Blavatsky, Denis Wheatley and—I am pretty sure—Czech magician, Franz Bardon. I even started attending a group at the local Methodist Church called the Church for Spiritual and Psychical Research at the age of twelve. There wasn't a soul there under fifty-five except for me.

I have continued to investigate the paranormal and the occult. Of course, many things have changed since I was a boy; the Internet, quantum physics, science… It's easier these days to gain access to both information and to people. Easier to discuss, talk about and yes – write about it. But when I was a six- or seven-year-old, I just knew things. I didn't get this understanding from those books, the Internet or TV. I got it from the ether and from my dreams.

In all honesty, I sometimes feel as if I know less now than I did then, and I know why. The world drags us in. It forces us to adapt, change, and become 'normal.' It places us in stressful situations where, if we conform, all is more or less acceptable; whereas, if we fight to be who we truly are, we get into trouble. In the process, we are told what is normal and what is not; what we should see and what we shouldn't; what exists and what does not.

So, there you go. I would like to re-learn what I knew when I was a small boy; to relearn how to be a child and to imagine with total clarity and see the hidden things—the magical things—that exist all around us.

This book contains creepy tales of spine chilling happenings, some of which happened to me, and many of which happened to others around me. There was a time when I would share my experiences and hear those of others in return. Almost everyone has a scary story. This book contains a collection of our stories—the ones I remember because they were creepy or strange or both. The truth is stranger than fiction they say, and the stories in this book will make you understand that nothing is a truer statement than that.

A last word, though. Evil is the opposite of good just like light and dark, or heads and tails. These things are just the opposite of the other. For one to exist, the other also must exist. Evil lurks just as surely as the darkness falls each and every night when the sun sets. If there is *this* side where we all are now, then surely there must also be the *other* side? And who knows what nightmares lurk there waiting for their opportunity to scare you!

The Importance of Asking Questions

Why do men have nipples?

Why don't Czech men know about deodorant?

Why is GOD DOG spelt backwards?

Why does Wayne Rooney get paid so much money?

What happened to Trilobites?

It's these sorts of questions—ones for which there are really no definitive answers. I hate questions with no answer. I detest not knowing. There seems to be little point in a question if there is no answer.

My favorite question is *'What am I?'* I see and interact with a world that I sense, but at times of perhaps total lunacy, I entertain the idea that it is my world. There is only me and everything is me. Perhaps this sounds arrogant, but I don't mean it that way. There is just a gulf between the real (me) and what seems to be real (the world) that confounds me.

I have always thought like this and asked those questions. Even as a child I asked, *'What am I?' 'Why am I here?'*

Not being able to answer these questions literally drives me mad. I cannot stand not knowing what the hell everything is. It must be something, surely, but why? And how? See! Questions and yet more questions.

We must always ask questions and contemplate even if there is no answer. In the quiet contemplation of the question, images and thoughts arise spontaneously as insights. We may not ever answer the question itself, but we can pry open some other secrets along the way.

The paranormal is one of those questions. *What are ghosts? Do they really exist? Or are they just in our heads?*

Let's explore a bit and see.

Medium

There was a time growing up when I became quite fascinated by spiritualism. The idea that a person could communicate with the dead—actually see and hear ghosts—was of great interest to me. This was an interest that my mother was actually willing to share with me, and so we ended up taking a couple of trips to a spiritualist church in Hull, England. These sessions were always characterized as demonstrations of clairvoyance, rather than speaking with the dead; but that is exactly what these people did.

On our second trip, my dad decided to stay at home, muttering something about it 'only encouraging weird activity,' but he was always interested in what had happened at the meetings, of course. He was, I believe, quite right. It did encourage the strange, ghostly activity that was going on in our house at that time, and it also made me more open to strange phenomena.

Attending a spiritualist church as a teenage boy was interesting in and of itself. The first thing I noticed was that the vast majority of my fellow visitors were female and well over the age of fifty. However, by contrast, the mediums were often younger people. That evening, it was quite a full audience for the demonstration as the medium was highly regarded, and he apparently attracted a more diverse audience. He was two or three readings into the evening when his eyes met mine.

"Young man," he said.

I gulped and likely flushed, as all eyes suddenly stared at me.

"I have a man here with me in spirit who would like to warn you about that motorbike that you have. He is showing me that you will have an accident, so be careful. He is young, this man, and he is wearing motorcycle gear. He passed some time ago, though," said the medium.

To be honest, I could barely speak. I just nodded acknowledgement, and the medium duly moved on to his next 'victim.'

Of course, I was consumed with my own thoughts for the rest of the demonstration. We thought that the young man could have been my dad's brother who had died long before I was born in a motorcycle accident; and yes, I had just recently bought a second-hand Honda C70 motorbike.

At the end of the meeting, both the medium and the organizer approached my mother and me. The organizer knew us and lived in the same area that we did. It transpired that the medium wanted to spend some time with me. He said that he had some things he wanted to tell me, and so, could I come by the next day around 2 p.m. for some tea?

We went home and told my dad what had occurred. He was understandably a little upset at the idea of his brother coming through, but he agreed that I should go for the tea and see what the medium had to say.

The next day was actually very disappointing at the time. I had fostered this idea that somehow the medium would tell me something really important, meaningful and deep. In fact, we simply sat in the backyard drinking tea and eating cakes, just chit chatting for about an hour or so. After that, the organizer suggested I should leave so as not to tire the medium, who would be giving another session later that day.

As I was about to leave, however, the medium looked at me and said, "Do you write at all, Gary?"

"Not much. Why?"

"Well, I just wanted to say that you will one day write a lot."

"Okay, thank you," I replied.

"One more thing, Gary."

"Yes?"

"Be open."

"I'm sorry?" I asked, somewhat puzzled.

"Be open to spirit. They will write through you. Don't be afraid. It will feel quite natural. It may not happen for many years yet, but it will, and I think that you might just sit from time to time with a pen in hand and a bit of paper and see if it happens."

"Thank you," I said again, feeling a bitter sense of disappointment. Was that all?

Apparently, the medium put on an uncharacteristically poor showing later that evening. He was tired from meeting with me, he had claimed. I didn't understand why that should be so, nor really why he wanted to meet with me. At the time, I didn't believe that he had told me anything very much of value at all.

About six months later, I visited the University of Hull. They had an open day for prospective students. I was seventeen and looking forward to going to university, so I went. Driving back home on my motorbike, as I accelerated away from some traffic lights, I suddenly saw a blur jump out in front of me. I braked as hard as I could, but I hit whatever it was. I heard the yelp of agony as I did so, and then I found myself sliding along the street at about 30 mph, until the handlebar hit a pothole and threw me away, gashing a hole in my knee as I went. The bike was messed up, I was okay (although bruised and bleeding), and the poor dog was dead. I felt bad. I felt terribly guilty for killing a dog. I also felt very fortunate that the light had turned red behind me, and I wasn't run over by a car.

I remembered the medium then—what he had said in the message—and I understood that this was a sign.

Now, I do indeed write. I write a lot. And the spirits? Well, they do come through. As the boy in the movie said, I see dead people.

Footsteps in the Night

We had all looked forward to the family holiday for quite some time. Two weeks in a large, rented mobile home on a picturesque camping site in Brittany located right on the banks of a river and also by a quality beach. My brothers had prepared their windsurfers, and now all we needed was good weather for a brilliant vacation.

The campsite was really nice. It was set in a lush forest that sloped down to a river. The river was filled with crystal clear, greenish water at high tide, and at low tide, the wet, rippled sand and occasional rocks lay revealed in the sun, while just a small trickle of water ran through the middle of where the river had been. It was ideal for windsurfing and also for a spot of evening or morning fishing. Just a few hundred meters downstream, the river opened up into the ocean and a magnificent white sandy beach. The mobile home was well-equipped and large. My parents had the back bedroom, my brothers had another bedroom and me? Well, I used the make-up bed in the dining area.

There were lots of other teenagers on the site, and we would play ping-pong and drink cold Oranginas at night, while listening to the music on the jukebox. There was a girl there that I liked, too. All seemed set for a great vacation.

Awakening that first morning, we set about a breakfast of French baguette, ham and cheese. The sun was shining, and we were all keen to get to the beach just as soon as possible.

"Gosh, someone was walking up and down the caravan a lot last night," said my dad. "Who was it?"

We all looked at each other quizzically, but none of us could recall anything but sleeping. We dismissed his comment, and off we went to the beach for a day of sea, sand and surf.

That night, I was the last in and also last to bed. Being the eldest and in my late teens, I had a bit more leeway than my brothers, and I was quite keen to spend time with the girl I had just met. I entered the caravan quietly, undressed in the dark, and got into bed. Not a few moments afterwards, I heard footsteps in the caravan. I sat up expecting to see one of my brothers. There was no one. *Perhaps it was something walking on the roof – a bird, maybe,* I thought, as I rolled over and tried to sleep. It happened again, though—distinct footsteps running up through the caravan. I sat up and reached for the light. Again, there was no one there.

At this point, I began to feel an icy shiver run down my spine, and the hair on the back of my neck stood up on end. Could it be that whatever was in our house back home had followed us here? At home, I had been experiencing footsteps, sighs and poltergeist activity on and off for a while. I was pleased to go on vacation to escape from it. Had it followed us?

It took me a while to sleep that night. I kept hearing the distinct noise of footsteps running up and down the caravan. Or was it something on the roof? I couldn't be sure I decided, but I knew deep down inside that I could sense something unpleasant in that caravan.

The next morning, after a disturbed sleep, I told my dad and he nodded. He thought he had heard footsteps that night, too. My brothers had, as well. Dad went out to inspect the roof. There were no tree branches or anything obvious to make any such noise. No way for anything to jump onto the roof. There was a growing, unspoken air of trepidation among us that morning.

For the next several nights, we heard nothing. However, periodically during the vacation, we all heard, quite plainly, footsteps running through the caravan. One night, we thought we also saw a dark shadow. None of us discussed the matter for fear of encouraging whatever this activity was, until we were on our way home. I had spent most nights clutching a flashlight and burrowed down in my sleeping bag. We never saw anything other than that shadow nor did we hear anything else; just those running footsteps. On the nights we heard them, they would repeat over and over again.

A haunted caravan? Perhaps. We never really did get to the bottom of the mystery, but even now, when we discuss holidays or the strange events that happened to us, the strange footsteps and dark shadow are always raised by one of us.

A Night in My Life

When I was a teenager, many strange things happened, some of which I documented in *My Haunted Life*. However, it is difficult to really convey the terror that I felt at times as these events would unfold. There was one night that probably best exemplifies this. My parents and brothers had left the morning to go to France on vacation. The following morning, my uncle would be picking me up and taking me to the railway station in Hull to set off on a 6-week geological mapping project on the Scottish island of Eigg. I was alone for one evening in that house.

I started the evening by going out with friends for a few beers and was joined by a girlfriend who agreed to come home with me for a 'coffee.' She had no idea what that coffee would actually entail. We entered the house, and I made the coffee and took her through to the lounge where I put on the TV. Within a few minutes, it had started.

The sudden crashing noise caused my girlfriend to jump. She looked at me as if to say, *"What was that?"* I told her it was probably just something falling over upstairs, but when it happened again and then again, she became suspicious. Things may fall over once, but not over and over again! She noticed also that I was tense and scared. Who wouldn't be?

I told her then. I told her about the strange noises, footsteps, the movement of things around the house and so on. I thought she would freak out and want to leave, but she was braver than me and was actually fascinated by the whole thing. We sat talking about this, and I could feel the hairs on the back of my neck rising. It was getting colder and colder. It was almost as if the act of talking about it was making it happen more. There was another bang and a crash, and she jumped and then giggled at her own reaction.

She decided to stay the night with me—both to keep me company and also because I think she was intrigued. She wasn't frightened. Yet. We put on a record and played cards for a while. Periodically, the house would crack, creak and groan. Maybe that was just the house—maybe not. It was cold, very cold. At times, we could see the steam of our breath, despite the fact the gas fire was full on.

It got worse then.

There was a series of bangs followed by a short silence and then footsteps above us upstairs.

"There is no one in but you and me," I confirmed as she looked at me quizzically.

I think that is when she perhaps started to get scared, as well. She hugged me, and we sat in the middle of the lounge hugging and shivering in the cold.

The footsteps stopped, there was a large sighing sound, and then the footsteps began again and a few more bangs and crashes. It really was cold and getting colder. It was icy, in fact, and we shivered.

The lights flickered a bit and the footsteps resumed. The stairs creaked as something slowly and purposefully came down the stairs. With each creak, each sigh and each little noise, one of us would jump. My heart was beating so loudly, I could hear it. She buried her head into my chest as the steps finally reached the bottom of the staircase. The expectation of horror was now part of the terror itself. What would happen next? I knew. It was what happened every time.

There was an even louder sigh and then a step. The lounge door, which was almost closed, began to open. Slowly, it opened wider and wider. Suddenly, it flew open with a crash as it hit the adjacent wall. There was nothing there. There never was. My friend screamed, and I sprang up and charged towards the door, angrily shouting a stream of four letter words and telling this entity where to go.

Anger always worked. The house fell quiet. It began to warm up. We fell asleep finally, holding each other propped up by the couch. I was pleased she had stayed. I was pleased someone else had experienced it. I was amazed by her bravery. I was pleased to leave for six weeks the next morning.

The Chess Piece

A friend of mine once told me this story on a Halloween many years ago. It chilled me to the bone. Whether it is true or not, I am not sure, although he swore on his mother's grave that it was.

In the late 1970s, the central cemetery in west Hull was a real eyesore. It was overrun with trees, bushes and weeds, and it was used as a place for all sorts of illicit activities. Most people gave it a very wide berth indeed. Many of the graves in the cemetery are Victorian, and they are grandiose monstrosities of a bygone era. It is a pretty damned creepy place in fact. These days, the whole area has been cleaned up, tidied and is actually worthy of a visit. However, back then, it was a place to be avoided if at all possible.

My friend was walking home, somewhat tipsy, from the pub with a couple of other friends that night in the late 1970s. They thought it might be scary fun to take a trip through the cemetery. Who wouldn't? They decided to walk across it, and while picking their way between overgrown and fallen tombstones, heavy undergrowth and trees, to their horror, they came to an area where many of the graves had been tampered with. Whether for theft or some other macabre reason, in this area in the middle of the cemetery lay scattered bones and open graves with coffins and contents partially exposed. Horrified, the three friends began to hurry, totally creeped out by the place and what they saw there.

This is where it gets interesting, however, because at this point, my friend accidentally kicked something as he moved as swiftly as possible through this darkened field of bones. To his utter horror, he realized that it was a human skull as he watched it rolling away into the undergrowth.

He told me that in a moment of pure madness, he decided to take it with him. Gingerly picking up the skull, he ran with his two friends to the nearest way out of the creepy cemetery. Having escaped from the cemetery, he stuffed the trophy skull in his bag, and they all went home.

When he arrived home, he took out the skull and examined it. It grinned back at him and was in good condition. He was actually quite proud of his fearlessness and, with some satisfaction, he placed the skull on his bedside table for further inspection and cleaning the next morning before he passed out to sleep.

Awakening the next morning, instead of the skull that he and his friends had collected the night before, he was shocked to find a large, carved ivory chess piece sitting on the table. The chess piece was carved in the form a man. This freaked him out no end. Where was the skull? Where had this come from? He later confirmed with his mates that he had taken a skull from the cemetery, but that skull was now a large ivory chess piece. The chess piece was even scarier to him than the skull. It seemed to have a dark presence around it and, after a couple of days, he and his friends returned it to where they had found it—during daylight. They left it back in the cemetery where they felt that it belonged.

Did the chess piece turn back into a skull, we wonder? Or did he simply imagine that it was a skull initially? We will never know.

Keeping Down the Dead

One of my college friends also had a night in a cemetery that he will never forget. He was fond of smoking the 'wacky backy,' but one night, he and his friends happened on some magic mushrooms. They were quite high already but still thought it might be fun to give the mushrooms a try.

Later, as he made his way home with two friends, he took his usual shortcut through the local cemetery. He really thought nothing of it. It was what he always did. He happened to notice that one of his shoes was untied because he tripped over it, and so he called on his two friends and then sat down briefly on a flat tombstone to refasten it.

As he sat there, he began to feel the tombstone move underneath him. At first, he giggled. It was funny that he would imagine the tombstone moving. Then, it moved again. This time, he didn't laugh. Instead, he called more urgently for his friends. By the time they arrived, he was already laid face down on the tombstone, trying to hold it down and keep its occupant in the ground.

"Help!" he screamed. "This one is trying to get out."

His two friends jumped to his assistance, sitting on the tombstone while it writhed and moved up and down. The three of them pushed and held that tombstone down all night long, terrified, until the sun rose and dawn broke. All three of them swore that the grave's occupant was trying to get out and that only a herculean effort had kept him in the ground where he belonged.

They all arrived home just after dawn, covered in sweat and white as ghosts themselves. Mushrooms were never on the agenda again and neither was the shortcut through the cemetery.

Death Sign

Many, many families lost relatives and friends in the Second World War, and ours was no different. My great uncle, a young and well-loved lad of just sixteen, went off to serve his country aboard a big steamer as part of the merchant navy. He came from quite a large and close family who naturally worried a lot about him. His older sister was my grandmother, and she and her husband and young children lived in west Hull. My great uncle was a popular and regular visitor, and in reality, wasn't much older than his nieces and nephews.

When he went off on his first voyage, I suppose there was much excitement and perhaps a little fear on his part and that of the family in general. It must have been quite an adventure to join the merchant navy and then set sail for some far off destination.

One night, several weeks into his maiden voyage, the entire household was awakened by a tremendous crash. Granddad, a very pragmatic man and a baker by trade, got up. With flashlight in hand, he checked the house from top to bottom looking for whatever it was that had caused the crash and had awakened the entire household. Finding nothing, he reassured the family, and they all duly returned to bed.

Of course, back in those days, news took a long time to travel, and it was several days before the telegram actually arrived, but arrive it did. Great Uncle would not see his seventeenth year, as his ship had been sunk, with all hands lost, by a German U-boat. As the family mourned and sought out more information, they were shocked to learn that the ship actually sank in the early hours of the night of the unexplained crash they had heard.

It was as if they, too, had heard the torpedo explode all those hundreds, if not thousands of miles, away from the actual event. It was as if my great uncle had signaled his goodbye to his family that night and gone out with a bang and a crash.

Meet My Guide

My father was a very good man and a great father. He was always so understanding of the strange events that happened to me and us while I was growing up and even into adult life. The reason for this was that he, too, experienced strange things and had done so since he was a boy. In fact, his mother was a medium, and my dad plainly had inherited some of the gift (?) and carried like an unwanted burden through his life. Unfortunately, Dad was a strong and quiet man, so he never told me much about his own experiences, but every now and then, perhaps over a pint, if he was in the right mood, he would mention one or two things that had occurred.

His memories begin with being a small boy and seeing his mother have many visitors. Eventually, his mother told him and his brother that she was a medium, and people would visit her to contact their dead relatives. He never said what he felt about that, but I can imagine it must have perturbed him at least a little. One day, he told me his mother started to tell her two young boys a little bit about being a medium. She told them that she had a spirit guide who worked through her and, if they wished, they could meet him. Overcoming any trepidation, my dad said yes, he would like to meet his mother's guide.

What happened next, though, was so unexpected and so shocking for a young mind that he remembered it vividly all of his life. His mother closed her eyes and began to breathe deeply and rhythmically for a while. He and his brother watched as her face and features slowly began to change. The eyes began to slant, a long and thin moustache and beard started to grow, her hair began to straighten and skin color change. In just a few moments, the two deeply horrified boys were looking, not at their mother, but at an old Chinese man who smiled back at them from where their mother's face had been.

One can imagine the fear and shock of this. Where was their mother? And who was this Chinese man? I know that it deeply disturbed him and that he had nightmares about it. I asked him why his mother did this, and he said that he thought she just genuinely wanted them to see there was nothing to be afraid of and hadn't realized how the boys would react. Anyway, it must have been a deeply traumatic experience for him.

Throughout his life, Dad plainly saw and heard things that others did not. Periodically, he would wake up, shouting and pushing some unseen thing away. When I asked him about this, he told me they were dark shadows and that was all he would ever tell me. Undoubtedly, he heard and saw some of things that I did growing up as he simply accepted what was going on and tried to help me.

It was my dad who told me one time that in his experience, getting angry worked. What he meant by this was that whatever these things were, they seemed to get stronger the more scared you were. They fed off the fear energy that they caused, and it was this energy that attracted them. He told me, "Get angry, swear and shout at them if needs be, but be angry. Don't let them feed off your fear." He was right. The strategy always worked since in some way, the anger overcame the fear, and they lost their energy source.

However, getting angry, while a good temporary strategy, isn't a long-term solution. The long-term solution required inner work. It requires a strong mind and will and the determination to not allow these things into your world at all.

Whispered Words

How would you react if, in the dead of night, you were awakened by cold breath on your face and someone speaking in your ear? Terrifying!

We were all excited. Geology fieldtrips were always fun, and the teacher was a great guy and turned a blind eye in the evening, allowing us to smoke and drink if we so chose. Many of us were eighteen anyway, and the few who were not, were just months away. It was a dark Friday night, gloomy and dark even as we left the school gates in the minibus. We chatted and laughed in the back, telling stories and jokes to pass the three or so hours it would take to reach the hotel.

At the hotel, most of us were allocated shared rooms, but one or two—we thought them lucky—were allocated single rooms. I was sharing with a friend, and we simply dumped our rucksacks on the small single beds and headed to the restaurant for dinner. He claimed the bed by the door. Dinner was followed by a few pints at the bar and then a relatively early night, as it would be a crack of dawn start the following morning.

At breakfast, I noticed one of my colleagues looked rather pale. He told me he hadn't slept so well, and after a little hesitation, he asked if I thought the hotel had a strange atmosphere. I hadn't noticed anything, and it certainly wasn't an old building or anything and so I told him I hadn't. The following morning, he looked even more haggard, and he asked me again about my feelings regarding the hotel (I was known even then for seeing ghosts and feeling atmospheres). I again told him that I had felt nothing and had slept very well.

"Then I have to ask you something, but please keep it quiet," he said, looking furtively about and speaking in a low voice.

I nodded.

"I know you will believe me, whereas others here will think me mad. There is something in my room," he said.

"Something like what?"

He looked uncomfortable and embarrassed and then said, "A shadow. When I am half asleep, it is by my bed. I feel cold breath on my face, and a voice says to me, '*Get out.*' That voice is a hoarse, whispering voice that sends shivers down my spine. I have never been so scared in all of my life."

I nodded now, paying more attention.

"At first, I thought I was imagining it, but it kept happening all night long. I haven't slept since we arrived and, last night, I kept the light on all night and it still happened. It is horrible. Horrible! I don't know if I will ever be able to relax again."

I didn't know what to say really except to reassure him that things like this did happen and that he wasn't losing his mind. I also told him that it most likely belonged to the room and wouldn't, as he feared, follow him home.

I went up to his room. He was one of the 'lucky' ones who got a room to himself. It was similar to our room, except smaller, but there was a definite atmosphere in the room. It was quite oppressive and one of loneliness and depression. If I were to spend much time in that room, it would drive me nuts. Being a bit fearful back then, I didn't want to stay in the room any longer than I had to nor did I try anything like contacting the presence. I simply told him that as we were checking out to leave, he should just mark it down to experience and try to forget about it.

It scared me too, to be honest. I could just imagine feeling a cold breath on my face in the dark of the night and hearing a disembodied voice tell me to 'Get out.' I would have done. Immediately.

Behind the Wall

Sometimes, it is better not to know.

For many years, he had lived in the small apartment in Houston, TX. Through all of that time, my work colleague had apparently put up with a variety of puzzling and increasingly scary phenomena. It had started with a periodic smell, like bad drains on a hot day. He had called out a plumber on one or two occasions since the stench had gotten so bad, but nothing was ever found that could be responsible for that odor. It seemed to emanate from the bathroom, and that's why it seemed likely to him that the drains were responsible. He put it down to the drains, and that was that.

A little while later, he noticed a damp patch on the wall in the bathroom. It wasn't wet—just damp— and over time, a dark green mold started to appear there. What was strange was that the moldy damp patch wasn't anywhere near to a water pipe or drain so far as he could tell. It was in the middle of the wall. It wasn't so bad as to make a fuss over; rather, it was just a bit puzzling. Like the smell, it defied a logical explanation.

It was when the scratching sounds started that he called someone in again. Perhaps an animal, a squirrel maybe, had gotten inside his wall cavity and was now causing untold damage there? The pest service, though, found no evidence of any animal or animal activity. Being a down to earth sort of person, he simply never thought it could be anything sinister. Not at that stage anyway. But the scratching noises continued and got progressively worse.

The final straw was the night when, entering the bathroom, he saw a shadowy figure standing there that disappeared the moment he switched on the light. It wasn't his imagination; he was pretty sure that he had seen a figure there standing in his bathroom. His blood ran cold, and for the first time, he began to be afraid. The smell, the damp patch, the scratching sounds, and now, a ghostly figure. He resolved to investigate.

In the morning, he found a large hammer and attacked the wall in the bathroom where that damp patch was. He was fearful of what he might find there and expected the worst. The plasterboard was easily smashed, and it didn't take him long to put a huge hole in the wall. As he did so, the rotting drains smell overwhelmed him. He shone his flashlight in the wall cavity but could see nothing to explain the damp patch or the smell. He took more of the wall down, now determined to get to the bottom of the mystery. At the bottom of the wall, he saw something. He carefully fished for the object. As he pulled on the rag he had found, he heard something heavy drop to the floor.

The rag was quite old but soiled almost certainly with blood. He put it to one side, and using his flashlight, peered again inside the wall cavity. Something glinted in the light of the flashlight, and he immediately knew what it was. A gun. He carefully fished out the handgun and realized that it had been wrapped in the rag. He called the police.

Although the police were unable to link the gun with any crime in their database, it was almost certain that the stain on the rag was human blood and that the gun wrapped in a bloody rag had been hidden in the wall cavity. The activity stopped once the gun was discovered, but the mystery remained. Who had hidden it there and why? And why had there been paranormal activity around the site of a hidden weapon?

We will never know.

Electrical Fault

A friend of mine at college moved into a new flat at the beginning of term. It was a nice, big, well-equipped flat too, and the rent was almost too good to be true. After a month, he moved out again. Here is why.

Over a beer or two, he told me that the place simply seemed too good to be true. The price was too low for such a nice place so conveniently located. However, he took it and counted his lucky stars. At first, all seemed fine and dandy. Periodically, however, especially around pub throwing out time, the doorbell would ring. He would go to the door and find no one there. Given the time of night it usually occurred, he put it down to drunken and playful neighbors.

Over the next two weeks, his neighbors began to play this trick at other times, too; and when it started happening in the early hours of the morning, he felt it was time to keep an eye out and complain. He saw one of his neighbors in the corridor the next day and asked if perhaps it were him playing the trick or perhaps they knew whom it might be. The neighbor, an older man, simply stared at him and said nothing at all. My friend thought this quite odd behavior.

When the owner arrived at the weekend as arranged, my friend was really getting quite angry. Several sleepless nights had put him in a foul and angry mood. He wanted this tomfoolery to end and end now, and he told the landlord this as they stood in the kitchen, drinking coffee. The landlord went slightly pale as his new tenant explained the problem. He put down his coffee and said, "Come with me, will you."

He led his new tenant to the front door and opened it and then said, "Ring the doorbell, please."

My friend pushed the small, round button as he imagined the practical joker in the building might have done. However, the bell did not ring.

"You see, the bell doesn't work. It hasn't worked in a long time because we unwired it."

My friend sucked air like a fish in bowl as he took in exactly what he had just heard... and then he understood.

"You mean, there is no bell?" he asked as if to make sure.

"There isn't and hasn't been a bell in a long time," said the concerned landlord.

Unsurprisingly, my friend immediately moved out.

The Watcher

In recent years, black-eyed kids have become something of a phenomenon, but similar things have occurred in the past, too. At a meeting of some very religious Christians to which I was taken by a family relative, I found myself taking part in one of those late night, around the bonfire, ghost and scary story telling sessions. I was truly surprised that these teens, on a weekend retreat with an evangelical group, would be interested in such tales. However, one of the tales really caught my imagination and scared the hell out of me.

One of the girls told us how growing up in their house in the English countryside, she would often have that very bizarre feeling that she was being watched. There was never anyone there, of course. It was just a strong feeling and nothing more. However, one evening as she closed the curtains to her bedroom, she saw a figure standing some distance away in the back garden. It was a shadowy figure in the evening dusk and some distance away as their back garden was very large so she could not make out any detail. She dismissed it more or less immediately as nothing.

A few nights later, as she closed those curtains she again saw the same figure standing there in the middle of the yard. It was just a silhouette. This time, she stopped for a moment and stared. *Who was it that was standing in their back garden again?* The figure then seemed to gently glide farther away into the shadows of the undergrowth at the back of the garden as if hiding itself, knowing that it had been seen. She was rather disturbed by this and went down to tell her parents about the intruder. Her father took a look around the back garden, but finding no one, he returned suggesting it was just a shadow or something and nothing to worry about.

Well, as the days and weeks went by, she began to see the figure more often. Always standing in the same spot in the backyard and always gliding back into the shadows if seen. The feeling of being watched intensified also. It began to scare her more and more. She started to sleep with her night light on.

The resolution of her story was also something of a surprise. A few weeks later, as she returned from school in the dark, she felt as if she was being watched. Turning, she thought she saw the shadowy figure gliding along some distance behind her. This new development scared her; but more importantly, it made her feel very angry. As she got closer to their house down the country lane, she suddenly turned and ran screaming as she went in anger towards the dark, shadowy figure.

As she got closer to it, she began to have doubts about her strategy, but she prayed for guidance and help and continued her short run towards this watching wraith. As she approached it, she noted that it appeared to have no real substance. It was like black fog. At the moment she entered that black fog, she thought she caught a glimpse of bright red eyes. She heard chuckling laughter, and then it was gone.

In fact, it was gone for good. She no longer felt watched and no longer saw the shadowy figure. She believed it to be a demon that had come to challenge her faith in Christ. Her faith had overcome it.

It was a compelling story and very scary to those with vivid imaginations and little faith.

A Glimpse into the Past

Sometimes, whatever is behind this Matrix in which we live has a disturbance, and if anyone is around to notice, something strange and sometimes scary occurs. On our many weekend camping trips, we visited many locations around east Yorkshire. There was one location that I remember in particular because of what one of our fellow camping fanatics told us.

The location was a small town outside of Hull in the chalk hills called the Wolds. At one time, the town had been the site of a shunting yard and a very long tunnel on the main railway line. By the time we visited, the railway lines had long gone, and the land had fallen into disuse. We visited the tunnel, though, and we walked the entire distance with flashlights to find the other end (over a half-mile away) blocked with barbed wire. It was fun walking through that brick tunnel and seeing the black carbon-stained roof and disturbing the bats that now called it home.

Later that day, we were telling some of our fellow campers about our exploration of the tunnel and the old shunting yard. He asked us how it looked. We told him that it was a pretty dilapidated and overgrown wasteland. He nodded and then proceeded to tell us the strangest of tales.

A previous year, he told us, the weekend camping had been in the same location organized by the local camping club. He, too, had decided to take a stroll and look at the old railway tunnel, and so he and a friend set off in the morning on the short walk to the shunting yard location. As they came over the brow of the hill and looked down into the shunting yard, they were surprised to see an engine there, throwing out grey steam and black smoke. The shunting yard was a hive of activity with men running around and wagons filled with supplies. They even heard the blowing of a whistle and the distinctive sounds of a steam engine. The two men looked at each other in total surprise and shock. There hadn't been a steam train on that line in years. In fact, there hadn't been a railway line there in years.

When they looked back down into the shunting yard, there was an overgrown piece of wasteland littered with piles of pebbles and stones for road works. No engine, no men, no smoke nor steam. They both sat down and discussed what they had seen, quite shocked. Each man had seen the working shunting yard initially. They sat for some time and then ventured down to the yard and to the tunnel entrance. It was now exactly how they had expected it to be.

For just a moment, had the two men looked back through years of time and seen a scene from the past? Had a glitch in the Matrix been experienced by the two campers? We found it a fascinating story, and I recall being rather jealous that it hadn't happened to us, too.

The Blue Room

One year, we rented a house in Wales for a week and invited my parents along. The house was a beautiful, old house in mid-Wales by the ocean that belonged to a friend of mine at work; but the house was haunted, and I knew it the moment that I saw it. Some of the events of that holiday are in *My Haunted Life,* but this tale centers around my mother.

Mum and Dad took a bedroom in the center of the house. After a few nights, they complained about their bedclothes being pulled away from them during the night. Mum, in particular, was quite frightened. There was a spare bedroom called the Blue Room, but it only had a single bed in it, and we told Mum that if she was frightened, she should move into the Blue Room.

Sure enough, that very night, she awoke as the bedclothes were slowly pulled from their bed. She had had enough, and she decided to leave Dad there on his own and head to the Blue Room just to try to get some undisturbed sleep.

She crossed the hallway and into the Blue Room, switching on the bedside light and climbing into bed.

Finally, she would get some sleep, she thought as she switched out the light. Unfortunately, the house had other ideas. No sooner had she settled down and gotten comfy, she opened her eyes to find the lamp back on. She switched it off again, and five minutes later, it switched back on again. Now, of course, she was afraid and could no longer sleep. She decided to leave the light on, but within five minutes, the lamp started to rapidly switch itself on and off over and over.

She was back in the other bedroom with my dad pretty quickly, and noise of my mum telling my dad what happened woke most of us up. We did try standing outside the Blue Room with the lamp on to see what might happen, but nothing did. Despite that, my mum swears the room was haunted and even reminded me of this incident just this week on the phone.

My dad thought it funny as I recall. It was just one more strange incident that occurred at that old family house in Wales, and one more reason why we never returned.

The Thing in the Basement

I have never had a house with a basement, but many older homes in the northeast of America have basements, and this is a story I heard from a work colleague while visiting New York on a business trip a few years ago. Over a beer, we had been discussing recent news stories of a strange beast in Texas and Mexico called the Chupacabra. This is a dog or raccoon-like creature that kills goats and other animals and drinks their blood. It was at that point that my friend told me the following story.

In his late teens, he and his family had moved to a small town somewhere in New York State. The house was in the countryside, and it came with a very large basement. The house was very picturesque and located in a really nice spot, and he and his family were happy to move there with their pet dog, who would now have lots of space to run around.

It was actually the dog that first alerted the family to the fact that something about the basement wasn't right. It would often smell around the doorway to the basement and get all excited, rushing down the wooden steps as soon as the basement door was open, wagging its tail furiously. That is until one day when it ran down into the darkness of the basement, and before anyone could switch on the light, came running back up with its tail between its legs, yelping. Of course, they investigated and found nothing that would cause the dog to do that. At the time, they really didn't think much about that incident; but later, they would think back and realize it was their first indication of the Thing in the basement.

The next incident was more puzzling. A neighbor had been hunting and shot a deer. He had given the family some deer meat and the father took the bag of meat down to the freezer in the basement. However, he was distracted for a moment. Leaving the bag of meat on top of the freezer, he returned up to the kitchen momentarily. When he returned to the basement, the bag of meat was on the floor of the basement and had been torn into apparently by a wild animal. He hunted around, looking for signs of a wild animal but found nothing at all.

So when scratching and scraping sounds were heard in the basement a little later, the assumption was that there was some kind of animal in the basement.

The family again searched the basement but found nothing at all, and yet the sounds were often heard when opening the basement door. It would go silent when the light was switched on. At this point, no one was scared at all. It was just aggravating that some animal had obviously taken up residence in the basement.

To that point, no one had seen the animal that lived in the basement. In fact, other than the bag of meat episode, there was no physical evidence of anything down there. No one ever found droppings or scratched surfaces or anything to indicate something physical was living down there. However, no one in the family had really thought about it as an animate Thing until it was actually seen.

The mother was about to prepare dinner one afternoon, and she needed to go down to the freezer for some frozen vegetables. She opened the basement door and stepped onto the first step before even looking for the light switch. In front of her, down at the bottom of the stairs, she saw what looked like a small demon. It had blood around its mouth and seemed to be like a cross between a rat and a small humanoid. She screamed and ran. The

Thing did too. Yet again, they searched the basement and found nothing, but the mother would no longer go down there alone.

For a while, the family lived in an uneasy truce with the Thing. They heard it scratching, but no one saw it. Only the father would venture down into the basement unaccompanied, and he would often do so with a small caliber pistol just in case he had an opportunity to do some pest control, he said. In the end, it was this strategy that resolved the situation – sort of.

After a day in which there had been a lot of scratching noises, when the father opened the basement door—which was now permanently locked with a secure padlock—he found physical scratch marks and gouges on the other side of that door. This was a worrying development. As he descended the steps in the dark, flashlight in one hand and gun in the other, he finally saw it. At the bottom of the stairs, he saw something that looked like a furry demon with pointed ears and pointed teeth. Its mouth seemed bloody, and its eyes gleamed back at him. Instinctively, he fired a shot followed by several more. Whatever the Thing was scuffled past him on the stair, through the kitchen and out into the twilight. My friend claimed to have seen it too as it ran through the kitchen. It was just a Thing. Rather like the Chupacabra, it defied description.

It seemed as if it had been hit as there was blood on the stair; but the good news was it had gone. Whatever it was, it no longer lived in their basement.

Playful Nature Spirits

Not all paranormal experiences are bad or indeed frightening. Some are positively uplifting, and so I would like to leave you all with a couple of positive experiences. Behind where we used to live in the district of Prague 6 is a beautiful valley. It is a place where many Czech folk go for long walks and bicycle rides, and it is the place where I would often walk at lunchtime for a break.

One such day as I entered the small muddy path that led down into the valley, I sensed something rather special. There was a very definite presence in the woods that day, and for some reason, it made me think of nature spirits and the Goddess. I asked Her and the nature spirits of the valley to be with me and to guide me in certain things that were taking place in my life at that time. It was such a beautiful day with magnificent leaf colors that ranged through yellow, greens and browns to red and the azure blue sky of an early autumn day. The sunlight sparkled in sheer rays of light through the treetops. The sounds of the gentle bubbling of water running down the small brook at the bottom of the valley helped to create a magical atmosphere. I was content.

But then, it happened.

At first, I thought it must have somehow started to rain as I heard what seemed like heavy raindrops hitting the leaves of the trees all around me; but instead of rain, leaves fell. The leaves swirled around and around as they fell down all around me like a snowfall of many colors. The gentle sounds that I heard were of leaf hitting leaf and it sounded like a gentle rain. At the same time, my other senses suddenly became more alert, and I could feel an energy developing in the vicinity. The back of my neck tingled, and I relaxed into that warm energy. The leaf rain moved, and I followed it. I marveled that this leaf rain was only in a single location, and it moved along the pathway with me.

I checked all around. There were no masses of leaves falling from trees, no breeze rustling the treetops and disrupting the leaves there. It really was centered just around my presence in the forest. I stood watching and began to laugh. This was surely a sign. My involuntary invocation had been heard, and a nature spirit or perhaps even the Goddess herself was playfully revealing herself to me. What a gift.

Even as I walked out of the forest and back up onto the road, the leaf rain seemed to follow. Not only that, but I became aware at one point of a small finch-like bird singing and watching me. Even as I passed not a foot underneath where it was perched, it did not move. I held my breath as I passed and turned as I walked to watch it in song. I stayed a while, and still it sang and watched me until I felt it was time to move on.

As I reached the crest of the valley, my dog ran ahead a little, and out of the bushes arose a huge bird. Not more than ten feet away, I watched, stunned, as a huge bird of prey took off and flew just inches over my head and out over the valley. I have no idea what type of bird it was, but I had never seen such a bird there before. Even now, I am wondering and in awe of this experience. It was an amazing experience of nature and a reminder that the Goddess is all around us if we will but look.

All Is One

I looked down onto and across a very strange and unfamiliar landscape. It was a rocky, largely barren place with sharpened peaks rising all around. Yellows and grays of the desert spread out beneath an azure sky. It was like looking into a vast amphitheater, and I recall thinking that the heat of the midday sun must be unbearable down there in the center. Strange, because 'down there' was really actually up there, on top of a flattened peak of sand and bare rock. It was a strange and crazy vantage point that I had of this scene. There were a number of squarish, whitened buildings dotted around in the yellow-green valleys—signs of life at least.

It was then that I noticed that atop the flattened, rocky peak in the center of my vision there were figures. From my position of vantage it seemed as if there may be a small crowd and three crosses. I recall idly wondering about the crosses until somehow I seemed to zoom in upon the scene as if to clarify what it was I was seeing. Sure enough, there were about fifty or so people gathered atop this mountain. Each wooden cross had a man upon it wracked in agony. The central cross was the one that drew my attention and that of the small crowd as a soldier thrust a spear into the man's side. The crowd gasped and cheered.

For me, it all happened in a rush as if the entire world had snuck in on me in an almighty rush of energies, sound and light. I realized clearly and without doubt that the Nazarene was dying, and as his head dropped and he gave a last breath, there was a massive explosion of light and energy. Momentarily, it was suddenly as dark as night; and then a small spark of light seemed to appear emanating from the Nazarene dead upon the cross, and this light moved outwards in a massive concentric circle, expanding and expanding to encapsulate everything. Again, my vantage point shifted and now seemed distant as I watched in sheer amazement at this concentric shower of light and energy spread through every rock, tree, living creature—every single molecule and atom on the planet.

I hadn't expected it, but the concentric ring of ever-expanding light seemed to hit me, and I was knocked back as if hit by a nuclear blast. The light filled me up. It enlightened every atom of my body sitting there in my office chair in Houston, Texas. A powerful rush of energy like nothing I had experienced to that point and have not experienced again. The effect of this was to momentarily knock me out—I blacked out literally. But then I was back.

I was everything. Everything was me. We were all one thing in total harmony. The planet, the Universe, you. It was all me. Us. It lasted for just an instant, and then the light was gone, moving off into the Universe in a huge concentric circle. But just for a moment, I had been fortunate to have the light of the Christ show me the Truth.

Closing Thoughts – Am I Alone?

I must confess that I often wonder if I am, in fact, alone. I mean, are any of YOU actually REAL? It seems much more likely that you are all simply figments of my furtive and overactive imagination.

Think about that for a minute.

The only thing that can really be real to each of us are our own experiences. Even those experiences are actually only secondhand, since if I touch you, it is my brain that interprets what that touch should feel like, and hell, what is 'feeling' anyway? It's something in my consciousness, and in my brain, and nothing to do with the atoms and molecules of my hand brushing against the atoms and molecules of you.

Our entire experience of the world OUT THERE (you included) is actually INSIDE OF ME. The whole world exists only in my mind, created there as I interact with whatever is actually outside of me. Every feeling, every sound, every sight is manufactured inside my consciousness.

You do not exist, people. I know it. I create you inside my mind and in my consciousness, but in reality, there is just me, and I am alone.

Perhaps this really is the Matrix, and in some other existence, I paid money to live in this creation and play this reality game. Having paid, was I then pushed into this creation for a while simply to experience something different?

Even though I awoke this morning and knew continuity in my life, there is no proof that yesterday actually ever happened at all, is there? Yesterday and all of the days prior could simply all be experiences programmed into my consciousness to give me a context for today. My memories were placed inside my head as a starting point for my day in the game of life.

So, am I alone and existing just for a day?

Think about it.

Well, if you actually have any reality outside of my consciousness, think about it and then get back to me....

Are you real?

Scared of the Dark

"Scared of the dark."

That's a funny expression if you really think about it. It's not so much that we are really scared of the dark but rather of what might be <u>hidden</u> in that darkness.

I know that growing up, and if I am truly honest, even now from time-to-time, I am afraid of the dark. I have had too many terrifying experiences in my life – some even shared with other independent witnesses – to discount the idea that, sometimes the dark is actually hiding something sinister and possibly even downright evil. These days, it is more the memory of my past terrifying experiences, that can have my heart palpitating, my palms sweaty, and the back of my neck hot and prickly! Now, I am able to consciously bring matters under control quite quickly, and that is usually all it takes to control my fear. I learned this technique studying magic. Mental discipline is part of the training of all magical systems and it is a fairly basic requirement to progress in magic.

I came to the conclusion several years ago, that many unwanted supernatural experiences were happening simply happening *because* of my fear. Whether you believe in the supernatural or not, supernatural experiences can be explained as either something feeding off of your fear or, it is actually your fear creating the experience in your head. It doesn't matters, because I believe both are the same thing anyway – everything that I experience, I create in my mind. This is why mental discipline is a key part of magical training.

These days, my fear of the dark is primarily a fear of what might be inside of me - in my inner make up - rather than anything that might be 'out there'. "Know thyself" is another part of magical training, and as we dig deep into our own psyche, we can meet aspects of ourselves we would rather remained buried deep in the darkness. However, we need to shine the light on these negative aspects of ourselves and try to balance them, if we are to progress as humans or magicians.

Perhaps the hardest thing of all is to be truly critical of our selves, and to recognize and come to terms with all of our flaws, shortcomings, and plain evilness. The Great Work of alchemy is the process by which we constantly boil and condense, heat and cool, wash and burn, the less than pure aspects of ourselves, seeking the transformation of these baser elements in to the pure gold that we should be. It is a lifetime's work as we are often quite oblivious to our own flaws, only recognizing them as we gain in life's experience.

The darkness is actually both outside and inside of us. I have come to understand and believe that the darkness inside is projected out into the darkness on the outside. I am still afraid of the dark because it hides things about myself that I have yet to discover, balance, or conquer.

Now, prepare to explore your own inner darkness, as I tell you more creepy true tales that will have you suddenly peeking behind you just to make absolutely sure that you didn't actually just see that shadow figure.

Did you?

Guardian Angel

I was told a number of strange tales by my brother's brother-in-law this Christmas regarding how assistance was often provided to him in times of need, prompting the question – does he, and all of us, have a guardian angel?

The first instance apparently took place one weekend as he took a ride on his motorcycle up into the north Yorkshire Moors. The moors are desolate and deserted, and the weather may change abruptly at a moments notice. They are absolutely not the sorts of place you want to be stuck in as dusk approaches, but as he reached the peak of a hill that afternoon, he realized that this might well become his fate. The engine of his bike began to splutter so he reached down to switch on the reserve tank, only to find it was already on. He was out of fuel and in the middle of nowhere.

He managed to coax the bike over the brow of the next hill and more or less free wheel down the other side before grinding to a halt. He was stuck in the middle of nowhere and he had no idea how far he might have to walk pushing his motorcycle to find anyone or anything. As the bike came to a stop, he looked to his left and out into the distance over nothing but rough fell and moor for miles and miles. The view in front of him was similar, as the country road wound its way across the gorse and heather of the rocky moors. He knew that behind him also were miles of similar road back to the nearest village. He looked to his right seeing a similar scene. This was not a great place to run out of fuel.

But wait.

He looked again to his right and noticed that on the dry stonewall opposite him was a red can. He stepped off his bike and pulled it back onto its stand. Inside his mind, he was busy calculating the very long odds that the red can actually had petrol in it. He reached the can and unscrewed the top. A quick sniff and he knew it was a gasoline can, but was there anything actually in it? He shook it and found it nearly full.

But surely, it can't actually be full of petrol? He thought to himself.

He stuck a finger in and sniffed the liquid on his finger. It was gasoline. He poured it into his tank and was soon on his way again thanking his lucky stars that, of all the remote places his bike had come to a stop, this one had a can of gasoline conveniently placed for him to refuel and ride to a gas station.

What where the odds of that? He wondered.

The second story took place in southern Ireland. It was late at night and money was low. He had to reach the north to make his way home, but what was his best bet? Should he try to hitch hike or spend his last few pounds on a train ticket? He decided to contemplate this question inside the railway station's waiting room. A quick check with the stationmaster confirmed what he had suspected; that he had barely enough money for the train ticket. It also confirmed that a train would be leaving for his required destination early in the morning.

He sat in the waiting room trying to decide what he should do. The stationmaster approached and asked him again.

" Are you going to buy a ticket? If not, you need to leave, as you can't stay here for the night. I have to lock up you see." He explained.

"Give me a minute to consider my options," our friend asked.

At that moment, a train arrived at the station and he watched as people got off the train. One, a smartly dressed man in suite and tie, got off the train and peered through the dirty glass door into the waiting room. Seeing someone was there, he opened the door and strode purposely over.

"Do you by chance need a ticket to Belfast?" he asked. "I have a spare one as I bought a return but only needed a single. I'd rather someone used the ticket if it were useful," said the man.

There it was. The answer to his dilemma. A free ticket to exactly where he needed to get and he would still have money remaining to buy some food.

"Why thank you," he said, taking the ticket.

The stationmaster came back in to the waiting room.

"Look, please make up your mind. That was the last train for the night and I need to lock up," he said gruffly.

"I have a ticket," he said waving it in front of the stationmaster. That gentleman just gave it to me."

The stationmaster looked at the ticket.

"So you do," he said scratching his chin. "OK, well the train is over there. It leaves at 5:30am so you might as well get on it and sleep. I'll lock the station up and you should be fine," he said with a twinkle in his eye.

Over the course of an evening, my brother's brother in law told me a number of very similar stories. In each, he was saved from a situation by a seeming coincidence. The work of a guardian angel do you think or is he just a lucky person?

The last tale he told us perhaps held a clue to this very question and is truly bizarre.

On this particular day, he found himself again needing a ride. As he peered down the road, he noticed a small car parked, but occupied, by the side of the road. He hurried along on the off chance that a lift might be had if the driver was going in his direction. As he arrived by the parked car, the driver who was an older gentlemen, called out to him.

"Hello there," he said cheerfully. "Glorious day."

"It is indeed." He replied.

"Let me ask you a question if you don't mind?" asked the driver.

He nodded.

"Do you believe in God?" said the driver.

What a very strange question, he thought to himself. However, it turned out that the driver wasn't going in his direction after all and so he resumed his walking pace down the country road. After a short while, he passed a small lake and, feeling rather warm, he decided that a quick swim would be a good idea. There was no one around and it would be easy to take a quick dip.

As he swam in the lake, he noticed to his amazement, a small boat heading in his direction. As it approached, the oarsman nodded at him.

"Gorgeous day?"

"Yes, beautiful," he shouted from the water.

"On a day such as this, you have to ask yourself about the God that made it all. Do you believe in God?" said the oarsman.

There it was. He was swimming in a lake in the middle of nowhere being asked for the second time in as many hours by a perfect stranger, if he believed in God.

How bizarre! He thought.

As he dressed and prepared to resume his walk, he noticed an older lady walking towards him.

"Hello young man." She said as she passed.

"Hello," he replied.

"What a simply beautiful day,' she said. "On a day like today you have to believe in God don't you think," she smiled as she passed.

What is the Universe trying to tell me? He asked himself.

What was it trying to tell him? Three perfect strangers in the space of a few hours and every one of them asked him about his belief in a God. But then, if he was really so lucky and, if so many coincidences occurred in his life, why wouldn't he indeed?

The Monster in the Cupboard

Small children everywhere are often scared by whatever monster they imagine is in that cupboard in their bedroom. Little Joseph was no exception. He had told his parents on a number of occasions that he didn't want to sleep in his room because the Thing in his cupboard might come out and get him. When his parents asked what the Thing might be, he described it as a 'dark teddy bear'. The house was relatively new and neither parent had any reason to believe this was anything other than a child's imagination at work.

Usually, children outgrow such fears and his parents expected Joe to eventually forget about the monster in the cupboard as well. However, he didn't. If anything, he became even more terrified of the cupboard as he got older and would often run headlong to his parent's bedroom in the night. His father, a friend of mine, would frequently show him that the cupboard was simply a cupboard filled with clothes. Joe would watch nervously from a safe distance, but remained unconvinced.

On his 8th birthday, Joe was given his first camera. It was a kid's camera, but it was quite capable of taking both reasonable photographs and also short videos. He was excited to have the camera and spent much of the evening playing with it by taking photographs and videos of everything in sight, including him self. For once, Joe didn't even seem so reluctant to go to bed and to his own room. This was surprising because Joe would usually do almost anything to avoid going to bed in that room.

His parents were very pleased that he went to his room, went to bed and stayed there with little or no fuss or argument that night. However, as usual, at some point early in the morning, Joe came running into his parent's bedroom and squeezed himself in between them. At breakfast, Joe's father admonished Joe who *'at the age of 8 really shouldn't be sleeping with his parents'.* Joe pulled out his camera.

"I took a photo of the monster Dad. You will have to believe me now." He said.

My friend took the camera his son was holding out to him. It was an orange plastic camera with blue buttons and viewfinder. The small display screen on the back was lit up and sure enough, there was a picture there. He looked more closely at it.

"It looks like a shadow?" he said looking at Joe.

"It's a monster Dad. It's a dark, horrid Monster and it tells me that it will take me away from you,"

Joe's father looked again at the screen. It was a shot from the bed towards that cupboard which was half open. A dark shadow was at one side of the cupboard. As he examined it more closely, he changed his mind. The dark shadow was peeking out from behind the cupboard door. *How could that be?* He said nothing, but instead focused Joe on getting ready for school.

However, when Joe had left, he looked again at the photograph. *There was something there – but what?* He went up to Joe's room and examined the cupboard again. He opened it. He played with the curtains and the lamps in the room trying to recreate what he saw in the photograph, but he could not. He began to feel a little uncomfortable. *Could it be that there really was something inside the cupboard?* He shook his head dismissing the thought and began to get ready to run an errand. It was then that he had an idea. It was a crazy idea but still, it would settle things perhaps once and for all. He spent the next 30 minutes setting up his own video camera in Joe's bedroom. He switched it on and left.

On his return a couple of hours later, he took a quick look at the footage taken. There was nothing just as he had expected. He chuckled to himself, as for a moment or two he had actually began to think that there might actually be something in the cupboard. However, he reset the equipment and let it run for another hour or so while he made himself lunch. There was no harm in being thorough he decided.

He returned after lunch to find the camera switched off. Puzzled, he switched it back on and reviewed the video. A quick glance showed nothing unusual recorded, just as he had expected, but just as he was about to switch it off and pack up the equipment, he saw it. A sudden and distinct shadowy figure emanated from the cupboard and a shadowy face looked into the camera lens just before the video ended abruptly as the camera was switched off. A chill ran up his spine. He rewound it. Yes, he hadn't imagined it. There was a shadow. Wispy, like smoke and it rapidly grew in size before the video ended. Shaking, he packed the equipment avoiding staring at the cupboard for the first time slightly afraid of what he might see.

Later, in the evening he reviewed the video with his wife. She sat wide-eyed in disbelief. Their son slept with them that night and every night thereafter until they had moved house.   There was, after all, a monster in the cupboard.

Proof

When I was a young boy, I recall having several conversations with my grandmother about life after death. I can only have been 8- or 9-years old, but the subject always fascinated me as I had had several such strange experiences myself. She would often say that, if there were an existence after death, she would try to find a way to let me know. I would always initially agree to this and then tell her I would rather she didn't. Fear set in, I suppose.

I had a very close relationship with my Grandmother and I had always wanted her to be at my wedding for some reason. However, by the time I got married, my Grandmother had already passed over to the other side. When we went on our honeymoon, I had a really strong feeling that my Grandmother was with me. I mentioned it several times to my ex-wife and as it turned out, it seemed that my Grandmother wanted to prove she was there after all.

I came in one day from the pool and took off my swimming shorts to take a shower. I hung the shorts on the shower door handle. When I finished my shower, the shorts were gone. I hunted for those shorts all over, but to no avail.

I went back to join my ex-wife by the pool and asked he if she had been in while I was in the shower. She said that she had not. When we returned together later that day, there were my shorts, right were I had left them. Of course, she thought this funny and assumed I had simply somehow not seen the shorts there.

Things took an interesting turn when she looked for the little white prayer book that her Grandmother had given her when she was a girl and that she had brought with her. We hunted high and low for that little book and not just once, but several times, to no avail. It had simply disappeared. I laughingly told her that my Grandmother was hiding it to prove that she was there with us. When we arrived home a couple of weeks later, my ex-wife went as white as a sheet with shock when she opened the case she had packed that morning. There was the white prayer book at the top of the bag as if it had been placed there on top of everything else.

Proof? That and the shorts weren't the only things to go missing and show up later where we left them or in another obvious place on that honeymoon and I do remain convinced that my Grandmother was giving me the proof that I had once asked her for.

Sometimes relatives do seem to come back to prove they are still around. My brother's friend also had a proof story for me when we met. His Grandfather lived in a small house by himself and he collected pretty much everything and anything and so when he passed, it was full to the brim with junk. He spent some time at the house sorting through things and, at one point was washing some pots in the sink, when there was five slow and very loud thumps on the pantry door. Our friend stood for a moment; his heart thumping, as he knew that no one else was around. When his initial shock subsided, he went to the pantry and opened the door. There was no one there and there was no other way in. He was forced to conclude that this was his Grandfather proving he still existed somewhere and in some form after death.

The Apparition

Growing up, I was in the local Church of England Choir. It wasn't so much that I was religious, but I did love to sing. The weekly schedule was a practice one night per week and then both morning and evening services on Sunday. It was paid work too, but the regular pay was paltry – just a few pence per quarter of a year. No, the big-ticket item was a wedding for which you might get as much as 50p!

Most weddings were held at the more picturesque parish church in a nearby village. This church was an old village church dating back to Norman times with it's own cemetery around it. I hated to go there especially in the dark winter evenings and even more so after hearing the story told by one of the other lads.

He had gone to sing at a wedding. It was after the service when he got changed and most people had already left the church. Only the vicar was there tidying up as he left. It was winter and by 4pm in the afternoon, it was already dark and gloomy. He recalled that, as he left the church, something didn't feel right.

As he walked down the short path from the church to the gate through the cemetery, he caught sight of the back of a woman. Actually, he first thought it was the bride from the wedding he had just sung at, as the lady was dressed all in flowing white. He could just see the top half of the figure over some bushes, but as he moved along the path and could see more, he was horrified to see that from where the figures knees should be down to the ground, there was nothing. He could see the tombstone behind her where there should be legs.

By now, his heart was beating rapidly and he stopped momentarily in fear. His flesh was crawling and his fear rising as he realized that the figure was turning its head in his direction. Somehow, he managed to unfreeze himself and run. He ran just as fast as he could down the path, out of the gate and didn't stop until he reached the local pub where he knew some other people were.

It was a long time before he agreed to do another wedding at the parish church.

Déjà vu

More or less everyone it seems experiences the phenomenon known as déjà vu. Usually, it takes the form of a vague feeling of having been somewhere or, in a certain situation before. However, for some, déjà vu can incorporate an aspect of parallel universes and an old colleague had had such an experience.

On arriving home from a trip one Sunday night, Greg suddenly had a feeling that he recognized as déjà vu. He had done this before. He paused in the moment of the experience and focused on it. He remembered having visited his aunt in a nearby town that afternoon. The shock of the memory was such that he had to sit down.

Suddenly, the events of the afternoon whizzed by his visual memory. The tea, the dining room of her home, the smell of baking mixed with the scent of freshly cut roses as a centerpiece on the dining table, the trinkets and ornate photographs of the family and friends laid out around the room, and the conversation.

It was the memory of that conversation that caused him shock. He had sat that afternoon and discussed his Mother's passing with her sister. They had, in sadness, recollected various events in her life shared with them both, together and individually. They had laughed at his Mother's habit of sometimes using wrong and totally inappropriate phrases, they had become sad at the manner of her death after a long and painful battle with cancer. It had been a long conversation of highs and lows celebrating his Mother's memory. As he sat there he could feel the heat of salty tears welling up as he recalled the details of the conversation and felt the shock of his Mother's passing once again.

For several minutes he struggled with this whole experience. He was confused. Very confused. His Mother was very much alive and she didn't have a sister, so what the hell was he recalling? So real was this memory that he had to call his Mother to check that she was actually still alive. Having verified this fact, he took a small whiskey and pondered what had just happened.

In his mind, there could only be one explanation. In some other parallel universe his mother did have a sister and she had just passed over. Somehow and momentarily, his feeling of déjà vu was a slip into another him in that parallel universe. There was no other explanation.

Orbs

As I have written these three *My Haunted Life* books, I have often noticed flashing lights and orbs floating around me. Orbs are often caught in photographs and cited as evidence for ghostly activity. I personally think most orbs are just particles of dust reflecting light from the camera flash to be honest. However, there are definite lights flashing around me when I sit and write these stories. They zip around out of the corner of my eye and attract my attention.

Many years ago, I also noticed this phenomenon around me. Back at college, these lights were often so numerous that it was like standing in a snowstorm. As a migraine sufferer, I did put it down to visual disturbances brought on by the migraine however, imagine my surprise when one day, the friend I was with looked at me and said "This room is full of sparkling lights – do you see them too?" I wasn't scared by this demonstration, but it did bother me just by the fact that it was distracting.

A friend of mine whom I was discussing these orbs with also had seen them physically. He said he was at the computer one day and noticed three light orbs appear to the side of him. Unlike mine, that seem to flash by me and are gone, these three maintained their presence and began to float towards the door of the room that served as his office. He got up and followed them. As he did so, the orbs began to move faster across another room, through a door, into his hall and finally out through the front door! He was left standing in the hall, staring at the back of his front door trying to figure out what it all meant.

Occasionally, orbs are associated with other bizarre activity. I have heard people talk of orbs that talk to them and orbs that contain faces. The face in the orb I suspect, is just the mind's basic image recognition program going haywire - but the voice? Well, that would scare the hell out of me. Luckily, the orbs and flashes I have seen have so far been silent ...

There are several popular theories as to what orbs really are. The first is that they are dust particles as I said above. Some people believe them to be angels or spirits around us, while others believe they are little packets of energy being attracted by an entity that is attempting to manifest itself on the physical plane. The friend who saw the lights with me that time told me that they were angels looking after me. Actually, I prefer the last theory in that it is energy associated with attempted manifestation. The fact I am sat here thinking about ghosts and the paranormal as I write, probably attracts entities to me and their presence is betrayed by these flashes of light and floating orbs that I see around me.

By the way, over your shoulder right now, there is a huge glowing orb.

The Face

Alan and John had decided to be brave. They had left home after work on the Friday night with a mission in mind; to visit an old abandoned holiday home they had discovered by the lake in a forest a few miles north of the Woodlands. They had an idea that it might just be fun to spend the weekend there and so they had packed their sleeping bags and camp cooking gear, and jumped in the car for the drive a few miles north. On arrival, they had a bit of a hike through the forest to find the lake and abandoned house they had discovered last summer.

The traffic was a bit heavier than anticipated and so, by the time they reached the area, it was getting late. They parked the car and set off through the forest. Boggy in places, the thick undergrowth also slowed them down, as did the mosquitoes that attacked them in wave after wave. By the time they reached the abandoned holiday home, it was already dusk. The first order of business was to get out the mosquito spray and cover them selves liberally before they were eaten alive. Next was to explore the small house for a place to camp out.

The house had only a couple of rooms downstairs and a couple more rooms upstairs and the stairs were more or less in tact. Part of the roof was missing but one of the upper rooms was more or less protected from the elements. The house was built into a slope so that the top floor really was the ground floor at the back. The backdoor was at that level too. They quickly moved some of the junk around and found a place to set up camp beds. By the time they were settled, it was pitch black. After a quick meal, they got into their sleeping bags and drank through a six-pack of beer telling each other ghost stories. Gradually, they became tired and passed out into sleep.

Alan woke up in the early hours of the morning. A wind had got up and the old house was creaking and groaning in the breeze. The branches of trees and bushes scrapped and banged on the sides of the house as well. After the ghost story telling, Alan was somewhat unnerved. It was creepy and pitch black. He could hear a noise too. He could swear he could hear footsteps above the howling of the wind; too loud to be a small animal. He feared as to what it might be and where it was coming from. He reached for a flashlight and switched it on. He cursed as a he realized that he hadn't changed the batteries since the last camping trip last year and the beam shone a pale-yellow without any real power.

He shone the flashlight around. The room was strewn with debris. Old furniture and abandoned possessions littered the floor, and an old, partly chewed out mattress was leant against one wall where they had put it to clear some space. There was that noise again! He shone the flashlight in the direction of where the noise had seemed to originate. His blood ran cold as he saw a face leering at him in the dim light of the flashlight. He jumped and he shouted for John, who stirred and then shouted, "What the hell is that?" as he too saw the pale face staring in from outside. They both lay there; their hearts beating and icy shivers running down their spines. They stared at the face but it stared right back at them freaking them out even more. It was just a vague face in the near darkness, but it stared at them and it did not waver in staring at them. What could it mean?

For almost a quarter of an hour, the staring game continued. At first, Alan and John were literally freaking out and trying to understand who or what it could be. As the time passed, and no one played chicken their confidence rose.

"Who are you?" yelled Alan at one point.

There was no response. Another few minutes passed and the ghostly face still looked in at them. Finally, Alan decided to be brave. He struggled out of his bag and ran screaming with waving arms and the flashlight towards the apparition. At the last minute, he stopped and turned to John letting out a yell.

"It's an old bloody mirror!" he shouted. "It's my bloody reflection in a mirror!"

The Lodger

The room was comfortable enough, but really nothing to write home about. It had a bed, a small bedside table, a wardrobe, and that was it. There was a shared bathroom in the hall. It would be just fine though, for the next several weeks as Jim finished the small project he had in the town. The family who lived in the house seemed friendly enough and the package offered a cooked breakfast and dinner each day combined in the weekly rent.

Arriving fairly late from the office on the first evening, he went straight to bed and slept like a log. He had got up at 5am and then driven the couple of hundred miles to arrive at his client's office by 9am. The combination of an early start, travel and a late finish to the day conspired to make him very tired.

At breakfast, Mrs. Tantum was very fussy, making sure the eggs were boiled to perfection and that the toast was warm. He ate in the dining room, which was a typical small, but pleasant dining room next to a kitchenette, and was filled with the usual bric-a-brac of family photographs and ornaments. Mrs. Tantum asked him a few questions about his family and general background and then disappeared to wash up.

He arrived back a little earlier the second evening and Mrs. Tantum invited him in to the lounge for a pot of tea. Mr. Tantum was already home and he made some sort of acknowledging noise from his armchair, but his eyes remained glued to the TV. Mrs. Tantum brought the tea and poured out two cups, one for each of them. She asked how the day had been and Mr. Tantum glared at her.

"Ignore him," she said. "Grumpy old sod just sits there all bloody night watching the box he does."

He made his excuses as soon as possible and went up to the guest room. The bed was made and his case was neatly laid out on the small table. He undressed and got into bed since he had really nothing better to do. He switched out the lamp and closed his eyes. When he opened them again the lamp was on. He switched out the lamp again. He opened his eyes to check he had done so and finding the room dark, rolled over onto his back.

At some time early in the morning, he woke up. He wasn't sure what had woken him but he decided he needed the bathroom. He got up in the dark and fiddled clumsily for the lamp. He found the lamp but then couldn't recall how it switched on and off and so he fumbled with it for a while. He heard someone pass by in the hallway and decided that must have been what had woken him. Finally, he found the lamp switch high up on the stem and the light came on. He peered out of his door hoping to avoid whomever it was walking around out in the hall. He could make out a figure in the bathroom and so he ducked back into his room and sat on the edge of the bed waiting for the flush to signal that it was OK to try again.

After about five minutes, he decided to take another look. The figure was no longer there and so, relieved, he made his way to the bathroom closing and locking the door behind him. Having finished his business, he unlocked and opened the door. He inadvertently jumped as he opened the door to find Mrs. Tantum standing there in a purplish dressing gown.

"Oh, sorry to make you jump," she said.

They navigated carefully around each other and Jim was relieved to get back to his bed. His switched out the lamp and was soon asleep.

The next morning, Jim apologized for his shock when opening the bathroom door. Mrs. Tantum laughed.

"Well, I didn't mean to scare you, just I had been waiting for ages for you to finish in there and I was just about to knock on the door to see if you were OK," she told him.

"Oh no," said Jim between bites. "That wasn't me. I waited about 10 minutes too for someone in the bathroom to leave."

Mrs. Tantum stopped what she was doing momentarily and half opened her mouth as if to say something but didn't. Jim could swear she had blushed too.

By the time Jim was back again, he had more or less forgotten about the whole thing. He had had a couple of beers after work with his client and felt just a little tipsy. He decided to go straight to bed rather than sit in the living room with the Tantum's. As he entered the door, he saw Mrs. Tantum at the top of stairs just about to disappear around the corner so he slowed his progress, hoping to avoid meeting her. He followed her up the stairs after a moment and on entering his room, closed the door.

He took off his coat and then peered around the door. He needed the bathroom again after the beer. He cursed silently as it appeared Mrs. Tantum was in there. He waited in his room for five minutes before peering out again. She was still there! He was by now jigging from one leg to the other and desperate. Desperation calls for bravery, he decided and so he left his room meaning to knock on the bathroom door.

"Ah hello Jim, good day at work?" said Mrs. Tantum's voice behind him from the stairwell.

Jim was confused. Who then was in the bathroom?

"I'm fine. Is Mr. Tantum in the bathroom?"

"Why no my dear, he is glued to the box downstairs as usual," she replied.

"Then..... who is?" he asked his voice trailing away a little.

"No one," said Mrs. Tantum looking past him to the bathroom.

Jim swung around. The bathroom was empty and the door open. A shiver ran down his spine. *Was it the beer?*

"There was just somebody in there I am sure," he said more as a question than a statement.

Mrs. Tantum again seemed to look hesitant and slightly pink.

"I don't think so," she said. "There is no one else in the house."

Jim was now puzzled and slightly creeped out, but he needed to go and so he did so. The bathroom certainly didn't look as if anyone had used it but there was a slight smell of male after-shave.

Jim went straight to bed. He lay there thinking but hoping to fall asleep. After a while he woke up – or he thought he did. It was dark as the hall light was off and everyone must be in bed except that he could hear loud whispers coming from downstairs. It was aggravating to say the least. He rolled over but the whispering was joined by loud TV sounds. He got up, switched on the lamp and went to the top of the stairs. The TV sounds and whispering were gone. It was all quiet.

He woke up again a little later. Someone was using the bathroom again he decided, as he heard footsteps along the hall outside his room. But wait? He could hear the whispering again, but this time in the hall outside of his door. He got up again fumbling for the lamp switch. As the light went on, the whispering stopped. Now his heart was beating and he was, for the first time, afraid. *What the hell was going on?* He peered outside of his door. He could see a shadow in the bathroom. Someone or some*thing* was there again. His heartbeat was so loud in his ears he thought he would be deafened, but he started towards the bathroom door. As he approached the door, he could see through the frosted glass in the upper part of the door that the shadowy figure seemed to be standing over the toilet bowl as a male would do.

He reached out for the door handle. The door suddenly swung open violently and a swish of cold air passed by him freezing him to the core. He stood there scared witless for a few moments and then turned and ran for the safety of his lit room. Panting and shivering with fear, he stood by the bed. Whispering again, loud this time, outside the door. The door began to open slowly, agonizingly slowly, he watched the door opening and screamed like a baby.

"Whatever is the matter?" said Mrs. Tantum who seemed visibly shocked and clutched Mr. Tantum's hand.

Jim more or less collapsed down onto the bed in relief. He was visibly shaking.

"I told you," said Mr. Tantum to his wife.

"What the hell is going on in this house," asked Jim looking from one to the other.

"Why my dear boy, we have another lodger I'm afraid," she said in a monotone. "A ghostly one."

Jim sat downstairs drinking copious cups of tea for the rest of the evening. He had packed his small bag and he wouldn't be coming back. Mr. and Mrs. Tantum sat with him. They looked glum and had explained that every time they took in a lodger, another ghostly lodger would make its presence felt. Jim felt sorry for them both but he wasn't going to stick around to find out what was behind this phenomenon.

These Shoes Are Made For Walking

When the Doughton's moved in to the rental house it was with some relief. They had been looking for sometime and this house was the perfect combination of size and location. They had finally managed to find the house with just two weeks remaining on their existing lease as well. In fact, the house was so nice and so cost effective they could hardly believe their luck.

The house was semi-furnished which meant that it wasn't going to look too empty with their sticks of furniture. All of their proper furniture was still in storage in England where it would remain until their return in a couple of years. Having some extra furniture then was a bonus.

In the spare bedroom, one such piece of furniture was a large wooden closet. Mrs. Doughton thought it would make the perfect spare storage for her additional clothing and so she intended to use it. As she started to move some of her less well-used clothing into it, she discovered an old pair of black men's leather shoes in it. Her initial reaction was to throw them in the trash, but then she re-considered. They weren't their property and perhaps she should put them in a plastic bag until she could check with the owners? The plastic bag was then removed to the downstairs and placed in a cupboard by the front door.

That night was their first night in their new home for the next two years. They were thrilled and happy and celebrated with a take away and a bottle of wine by candlelight in the dining room. However, it wasn't long before they were interrupted by the sounds of footsteps upstairs. They looked at each other quizzically before Mr. Doughton went off to investigate. He came back shortly having seen nor heard anyone.

As they retired to bed and switched out the lights, they both jumped as a huge crash sound came from the spare bedroom. Again, Mr. Doughton got up to investigate and this time he came back looking pale.

"All the clothes you placed in the closet are a right mess," he said. "It's as if someone rifled through them looking for something."

Both were now beginning to feel scared. They held on to each other in the semi-darkness after the light was switched off. Another bang and crash followed by definite footsteps and on came the light. Their hearts beating and icy sweat running down their backs, they investigated the spare room together. There, they found the closet door open and the clothing scattered around the room. They looked at each other in horror. What had only moments ago been their dream temporary home was rapidly turning into their worst nightmare?

It continued like this all night. Footsteps, bangs and crashes, occasional moans. Every time they went to investigate, no one or nothing was there. They spent most of the night huddled together downstairs until they could leave for a coffee shop. Anything to get out of the house.

At the coffee shop, Mr. Doughton called the landlord. After several attempts he got through. He explained that it would be impossible for them to stay in the house under such circumstances. The landlord listened patiently.

"Can I ask a question?" said the landlord.

"Of course", said Mr. Doughton.

"When you used that closet in the spare room, did you find an old pair of leather shoes at all?"

"Why yes, we did," said Mr. Doughton somewhat puzzled.

"And you removed them I suppose?"

"Yes, we did."

"Put them back and all will be fine. Old Mr. Heldenburg doesn't like losing his shoes. We have found he goes looking for them if he can't find them and he makes quite a noise, as you have discovered."

After a short discussion, the Doughtons's decided to give the suggestion a try. It was such a cost effective and convenient home, why wouldn't they? The shoes were returned to the closet.

The Doughton's enjoyed a two-year peaceful rental, but they also left a note in the closet about the shoes for the next tenants.

Battle Cry

My Dad told me this creepy story several times when I was growing up. His childhood wasn't so great and so he liked to escape at weekends or whenever he could. His best friend, Jack, and he, loved to cycle, camp and hike around East Yorkshire and that's what they did just anytime they could. It was the years directly after the war and there was little traffic or other people to bother them.

One night, they pitched their small two-man tent in a farmer's field near Long Marston. They knew very well that, in the vicinity, many years ago, a battle had taken place there during the English Civil war – The battle of Marston Moor. It was partly why they were there as they both had a love of history as well as the outdoors.

They retired as dusk came as they were heading back in the morning and needed to get up early to allow sufficient time for the trip. Cycling all day is tiring and so they had no problems sleeping.

Around 1am, a hand shaking his shoulder woke my Dad up. It was pitch black. As he awoke he heard Jack's voice,

"Nev, Nev, do you hear that?"

Dad listened and to his amazement he could hear the thudding of horses galloping, men shouting and screaming and the clash of steel on steel. This was taking place in a thunderstorm and was accompanied by the sound of rain, thunder and huge flashes of lightening. He was horrified.

The two of them sat in the dark listening to what he described as a cacophony of battle sounds all around their little tent in the field. They dare not move. They dare not look outside the tent. They simply sat there wide-eyed with cold sweat dribbling down their icy cold necks listening to the sounds of a Civil War battle in a thunderstorm going on around them.

As soon as dawn began to break, the sounds faded. They got up, skipped breakfast, and got out of there as soon as they could. The field was totally empty when they finally summed up the courage to leave the tent.

The experience obviously had a big impact on him because he would often tell my brothers and I the tale of the night the Battle of Marston Moor took place. I think what had shocked him more was that, when checking up on the battle years later, he discovered that it did actually take place in a thunderstorm.

Is Life Just One Big Fat Lie!

One of the central themes of all of my writings – even this My Haunted Life series – is the nature of reality and the role that we may play in dictating it. Over the last twenty or so years (if not my entire life really) I have read, meditated on, studied and discussed this topic, and in the process, I have come to several conclusions. One of these is that I now believe that much of our world is an illusion.

It's easy to draw analogies with movies like the Matrix here, and I and others often do, but what I mean is a lot of what we think we know isn't real. It isn't truth or fact. I once said (and thought it was rather cute) –

"The more I think on it the more I realize that certainty is an illusion. The winner wrote history, the news is provided with a spin and other people are opaque. We know nothing for certain. It used to be that the Internet might provide information, but it too is now nothing but opinion and scare mongering. Nothing can be relied upon. We have to look inside ourselves for anything of value – anything that can be relied upon – but it too is colored by our ego and personalities.
So in the end, if the past is a colored view and the future a fancy, what do we have left?

Simply to live in the moment...

(The Mystical Hexagram, Vasey & Vincent, 2012).

Life is an enigma and I may never actually understand the answers, but I do know this. Everything that we take to be true is probably not. Let me give a few examples -

1. History – history is written by the winner and it reflects a perception or view of what happened. There are alternative histories for everything and the sad thing is, they are all colored by the same issue.
2. Education – Education is partly about providing certain tools – reading, writing, critical thinking, and analysis – but only in limited degree. The rest of education is essentially to 'brainwash' you with cultural normality's, cultural convention and to ensure you don't actually challenge the system. Most people accept what they are told as the gospel truth and never for a minute stop to think critically or analytically about things. In this way, the illusion is maintained.

3. Religion – While all religions are probably based on wisdom and spiritual truth, they are all and without exception, subverted to match someone's

political or cultural agenda. They become the basis by which people can be manipulated and controlled.

4.   On a more mundane level, the music or entertainment industry can be used to prove its all illusion too. Many singers can't sing (they use computer software now to ensure perfect pitch), many musicians can't actually play, and many live performances are lip-synched. It's all a lie (It didn't used to be). Actors and actresses public personas are creations and false often nothing like the reality. Show business is really all a show – an illusion – just like everything else in your life.

5.   You are bombarded day in and day out with messages – some subliminal and others in your face – buy this, eat this its good for you, holiday here and so on. The marketing machine uses our ability to imagine and visualize – a rudimentary skill though it is in the majority of us) and uses OUR magic making ability and equipment to have us make THEIR reality. Our magic has been hijacked!

I could go on and on but I won't. Don't ask me who THEY might be. I have no idea and I am not a conspiracy theorist – that's just another fantastical dead end. That there is a THEY – whether THEY actually know it or not, I am sure.

I also have concluded this. Given that everything turns out to be illusion and, that I cannot trust anything, then I must turn to the only thing I can rely on – me. Unfortunately, I have to first clear the 'me' of all the nonsense I have been conditioned with and am bombarded with daily. I must know my own mind. This is far from easy and may not be attainable at all, but I can make progress towards it and, in doing so, I can take control of my life and my reality. I can be a true magician and imagine my thoughts into reality. Of course, I also live in other people's realities too and I must learn how to interact with their parallel universes as well.

You know, if the outer world we call life is an illusion while the inner world is real then surely, the Kingdom of heaven is within us and faith – well, it can move mountains. It would also mean that we create our own ghosts!

Face in the Window

The single story home sprawled over a large area and included an attached granny house, making it even larger. No one used the granny house anymore and since moving in, the four-room dwelling was used only for storage. It would have been more or less forgotten about except for the fact that it was situated at the end of the driveway and so every time a car came up the drive, it looked straight into the front windows of the granny house.

The family had moved in several years prior. They made full use of the large and rambling home that was set on a large forested lot. The Granny house had been initially explored and then more or less forgotten. They had no use for it really but, if the truth was told, it had a strange atmosphere as well.

Originally, it had been built for the elderly parents of a previous occupant. Right next door, the parents could be looked after and an eye easily kept on them. Some of the original furniture and fittings still sat inside it, gathering dust, even now. Perhaps it was that that gave it the atmosphere?

It was quite late at night as he drove his car into the driveway and up towards the Granny house. As the headlights of the big old car swung around and up the driveway, he caught a flash of a man's face staring out of the front window of the Granny house. Lit up by the harsh lights of the car, the face looked stark and white. It was made even more bizarre by the fact that, whoever it was, was wrapping the curtains around his head. Essentially, it was just a head in the window. He felt a chill of fear surge through his body and the hairs on the back of his neck stand up.

Logic then took over. Someone was in the Granny house who shouldn't be there. He shut down the car and strode of into the garage to grab a flashlight and his gun. He unlocked the Granny house door and switching on the lights, he hurled himself into the front room where the person had been. The curtains were still swinging from side-to-side but no one was there. He searched the four rooms for the next 10 minutes determined to find the person who was on his property, but he found no one. The chill returned as he began to realize that he had just seen a ghost.

He didn't mention it to his family but it began to play on his mind. The experience had scared him quite a bit if he was honest. A few weeks later, he became convinced that some presence was in that small building.

His wife had got up in the night and gone to the kitchen for a drink of milk. As she walked into the darkened kitchen, the outside light flicked on shining through the kitchen windows. He had been duly called to investigate. The switch for that light was in three locations – inside the back door, inside the locked garage and one inside the Granny house. He could account for the fact that no one had switched the light on in two out of three of those locations. He recalled the face caught in his headlights and shuddered. He would investigate in the morning.

In the morning he did check the Granny house but found it locked and undisturbed. There was just that atmosphere. It was a sort of cold heaviness. It was both uncomfortable and also a little creepy. He found himself avoiding the Granny house and dreading driving up the driveway after dark preferring instead to park in the street. He was unnerved. The Granny house was bulldozed that summer. He preferred it that way.

The Train Ride

His head dropped as he once again slipped off in to sleep. Of course, he immediately woke up again, mentally cursing his inability to sleep on a train. He opened his eyes and watched the monotonous eastern European countryside flash by without really registering any of it at all. The carriage reminded him of old black and white movies as it was so ancient and yet, being first class, it was, he had to admit, somewhat luxurious. It had definitely seen better days though, as the carpet was threadbare in the six parallel locations where travellers' feet would usually sit. It was a carriage in which three people sat facing three other people except today, it was just him and five comfy looking, but very empty, seats.

As the train hurtled onwards he noticed that the carriage lights would occasionally flicker. *Even the electrics were showing their age,* he thought. Initially, he had searched for a power outlet to charge his phone, but the train must have pre-dated portable electronic devices and it had no power sockets. His phone had subsequently died about 4 hours into this 10-hour journey.

He fought vainly to keep his eyes open as the rhythmic bumping of the train over the tracks rocked him to sleep. However, the train was beginning to slow and a stop appeared to be in the offing. He woke up a bit and peered into the twilight gloom out of the window. The train stopped briefly in what he could only think of as a village station, as there was just a station house and a few other buildings dotted around. As the train lurched forward again, he was surprised to see that someone had gotten on board. The man opened the carriage door and taking off a long coat and hat, sat diagonally opposite him registering his presence with a brief and perfunctory nod of the head.

The heat of the compartment and motion of the train began to work its sleep spell again and his head nodded occasionally as he dozed. From time to time, he opened his eyes and peeked at his new neighbor. The man was dark. Black hair and darkened skin like many of the indigenous population of this part of the Europe. His lips were pale and thin and a sharp nose jutted almost comically from a flat face accentuated by a high forehead. The man stared straight ahead. He didn't actually seem to blink at all. As if aware of another's gaze upon him, the man turned his head and looked over displaying small green eyes. At this, our friend closed his half opened eyes so as to not appear to be staring.

After a few moments, he half opened his eyes again. The man was again staring straight ahead and again, he did not appear to blink. He was dressed in a dark coat, which seemed to hide a suit underneath. He was clean-shaven and his hair was slightly oiled and clung to his scrawny head. An image of an Eagle came to mind. A tall, thin and unblinking, Eagle-like, man.

The heat seemed to be growing thicker as the train now hurtled through darkness, rocking and swaying him from side-to-side. His eyes felt increasingly heavy and more difficult to keep open for any length of time. He felt his head drop and the movement woke him again but only momentarily.

At first, he wasn't quite sure what it was he was feeling. *Was he sleeping and dreaming?*

He was aware of a slight pain and wetness at his neck. He felt as if he were falling down into a long cavernous gap between rising peaks that looked like very sharp teeth. There was a strange lapping sound in his ear too. He struggled to wake up but was only able to open his eyes very slightly. The pale but swarthy skinned man was staring at him with those green unblinking eyes. There was a strange faraway look on his face. The man licked his lips. *Was that blood on his lips?* Strangely, at that moment, he couldn't care less. He simply wanted and needed to sleep.

For a few moments, he closed his eyes again and began to drift off but then he suddenly and with growing horror realized that the man sat opposite him had two very long and very sharp-looking incisor teeth. He opened his eyes; suddenly this time and stared across at his neighbor. The man flashed a smile back. Those teeth! This time he caught sight of those pointed white teeth and the man's reddened tongue and lips. Instinctively he raised a hand to his neck where he had felt wetness. He wiped his neck and looked at the dark red streaks of blood on the back of his hand. His heart was pounding with sheer terror as he watched the man float up off of the seat and across the gap towards him. The eyes, unblinking, stared into his, and he found he could not move nor speak as that mouth descended again upon his neck. He blacked out.

The jolt of the train woke him with a jump. It took just a few moments for his waking moment to become a scream as he jumped back. His heart was pounding and he was wet with sweat. In the next few milliseconds, he realized that he was alone in the carraige. The strange, Eagle-like, unblinking man with teeth had gone. His hand immediately felt for the wound on his neck. He wiped his neck with the back of his hand and looked but there was no blood. He checked several times with the same result. He then got up and almost ran out of the carriage and down to the bathroom where he could look in the mirror to check visually. No blood, no marks; just his pale, sweaty face staring back at him from the mirror.

A feeling of relief passed over him and he felt quite giddy for a moment. He began to chuckle and then to laugh as he realized the whole thing had been a bad dream. *It had seemed so real though*, he thought to himself. *So very real!*

He returned to the carriage and checked around. There was no sign of anyone or anything except for his own luggage, book and papers on the seat. It had been a dream and a bad one at that.

He sat down and relaxed feeling the heat envelope him and the movement of the train started to make him sleepy again. He let it take him deeper into sleep. However, the train was beginning to slow and a stop appeared to be in the offing. He woke up a bit and peered into the twilight gloom out of the window. The train stopped briefly in what he could only think of as a village station, as there was just a station house and a few other buildings dotted around. As the train lurched forward again, he was surprised to see that someone had gotten on board. The man opened the carriage door and taking off a long coat and hat, sat diagonally opposite him registering his presence with a brief and perfunctory nod of the head.

It's All Fantasy

It's proven, so it has to be true
And now there's not a thing that we can do
Yet another litany of lies
Pulled off in front of our very eyes
It's a free show, though
So we mustn't complain
Hollywood in real-life
Actors showing grief and pain
The news isn't so good
And we are all so afraid
Pulled in so many directions
Playing out this dark charade
Lies become truth become lies
Who the hell can really tell?
Stories and often, just rumors
Everything merges simply so well
But amongst all these sleepers
One or two still think and question
Suspect that they smell a rat
Don't swallow that suggestion
Remaining single-minded
Looking inwards and deeply
Ignoring all this bloody nonsense
Staying true; the free me
It's pretty hard to do

When the information
Becomes disinformation
Packaged lies for easy consumption
Easy meat and quite a treat
For the controlling factor
The Matrix men hidden deep
While humanity is still asleep

G. Michael Vasey's Other Books

The Art Of Science
Asteroth's Books, 2015
ISBN: 150846054X
Paperback and Kindle editions

A new collection of 25 poems by G. Michael Vasey. Free verse to enchant your soul from Succubus to The Creator's Smile, each short poem dwells on love, inspiration, life and reality. A bardic appreciation of life through the eyes of a mystical soul.

Best Laid Plans and Other Strange Tails,
BookSurge, 2014
ISBN: 1500889601
Paperback and Kindle Versions

A fifth collection of poetry and rhyme by G. Michael Vasey musing about the magic of life. From the mystery of The Story, through to magic of the Hexagram and the number 6, Vasey twists words and phrases to paint deliciously vivid images of how he sees life and everything.

Moon Whispers, BookSurge, 2014
ISBN: 1499364105
Paperback and Kindle versions

A new collection of 30 poems about life, reality and everything.

Poems for the Little Room (Reissued), BookSurge, 2014
ISBN: 1493783114
Paperback and Kindle versions.

G. Michael Vasey's second book of poetry supplemented by photographs by Gabriela Vasey. It combines images and poems that range from a humorous look at a Czech TV interviewer, Jan Kraus, through to stories of idyllic love - both for partner and daughter. The idea behind this book was that it would be ideal for that little room where guests only want something to leaf through for a short time! Hence its name...

Originally issued by Lulu in 2011

]
Astral Messages, BookSurge, 2013
ISBN: 1490312633
Paperback and Kindle Formats

Astral Messages uses poems and blog articles from - Asteroth's Domain - in a poetic discussion about reality and magic. From the opening ethereal beauty of "Astral Messages" to the humor of the questioning about "Why is life so dirty," this is a collection of 17 new poems. Each is coupled with a short article to strengthen and bolster the points being made. At the end of the day, we are all magicians willfully creating our realities, and Astral Messages demonstrates how this touches all aspects of our lives - yes, even our socks!

The Last Observer: A Magical Battle for Reality, Roundfire, 2013
ISBN: 1782791825
Paperback and all formats of eBook

The Lord of the Elements wants to change reality. He has enlisted the evil Zeltan to help him, and together they will try to recruit Stanley, a man gifted with incredible imaginative capabilities to help them, unless Edward and his friends can stop them. A tale of white and black magic, quantum physics and a plot that twists and turns...

Features a compelling foreword by Anthony Peake, author of Is There Life After Death? and many other best selling books.

The Mystical Hexagram: The Seven Inner Stars of Power (with SC Vincent), Datura Press, 2012
ISBN: 0984822550
Paperback and Kindle Versions

The book explores a symbol. Not from some scholarly or deeply complex perspective, but seeing it as a representation relating to life and living. The forces and pressures that are associated with the hexagram are, after all, the forces of life at both practical and Universal levels. By exploring and beginning to understand the symbol, we are able to learn and discover more about ourselves.

Weird Tales: Other World Poetry, Booksurge, 2006
ISBN: 141965277X
Paperback and Kindle versions

Weird Tales is the second book published by Dr. G. Michael Vasey, and it is a collection of poems or simply 'words on paper.' Thirty-one poems written over many years ranging from love poems to caustic comments on modern society. It's all there...

Inner Journeys: Explorations of the Soul, Thoth, 2005
ISBN: 1870450817
Paperback and Kindle formats
Foreword by Dolores Ashcroft-Nowicki

Inner Journey: Explorations of the Soul was my first foray into publishing my experiences. It is somewhat autobiographical in that it deals with why I had an interest in all things Occult and follows my trail to the point where I found the Servants of the Light. It then tracks my experiences of taking the SOL's first course over 5-6 years and provides some insights into what I learned. In fact, it was Dolores Ashcroft-Nowicki, the

SOL's Director of Studies, who suggested I write the book and who kindly provided an introduction, too.

Blogs

http://www.garymvasey.com

http://www.asterothsdomain.com

About The Author

With 14 books in print, G. Michael Vasey is an established author with notable contributions in poetry, metaphysics, and business. His first novel - *The Last Observer* (Roundfire, 2013) - was published last year and is a thrilling cornucopia of mayhem, magic and murder.

A Yorkshire man who has spent most of his adult life exiled to Texas and now the Czech Republic, G. Michael Vasey writes for a living as a leading analyst in the commodity trading and risk management industry. On the side, he writes poems, blogs, books on metaphysics and novels, all with a theme of life and the nature of reality. Much of his inspiration comes from meditation and music.

He is currently working on The Lord of the Elements - the prequel to The Last Observer - and another on the concept of the Fool in magic.

He Tweets at @gmvasey and blogs at http://garymvasey.com.

Printed in Great Britain
by Amazon